COLOR

A Stroke of Brilliance®

A Guide to
Color & Decorating
with Paint

Benjamin Moore® PAINTS

COLOR
A Stroke of Brilliance®

A Guide to Color & Decorating with Paint

LESLIE HARRINGTON, ASID, ARIDO, IDC
with JOAN MACKIE

Benjamin Moore & Co.
Montvale, N.J. 07645
New York Office, 511 Canal Street
Manufacturing locations in Newark • Boston • Richmond • Jacksonville
Johnstown • Cleveland • Chicago • St. Louis • Houston • Dallas
Birmingham • Denver • Los Angeles • Santa Clara
Toronto • Montreal • Vancouver

Published in 1993 by
Benjamin Moore & Co.
51 Chestnut Ridge Road
Montvale, N. J.
07645-1862

ISBN 0-9696483-0-8

Produced by B & E Publications Inc.
Suite 265
7025 Tomken Road
Mississauga, Ontario
Canada L5S 1R6

Third Printing

Printed and Bound in U.S.A.

PHOTOGRAPHS BY:
Front Cover: TED YARWOOD, Toronto, Ontario.
Back Cover: MICHAEL MAHOVLICH Photography, Toronto, Ontario.

Pages 13, 19, 20, 21, 22, 29, 33, 34, 36, 37, 38, 41, 49, 51, 52, 54, 55, 69, 75, 110, 112, 113, 114, and 116/MICHAEL MAHOVLICH Photography, Toronto, Ontario; Pages 30, 31, 35, 56, 73, 77, 111, and 115/TED YARWOOD, Toronto, Ontario; Pages 47, 58, 59, 85, 87, 94, 99, 100, 101, and 102/ BENJAMIN MOORE & CO.; Pages 62, 83, 89, 91, 92, 95, 96, 97, 103, 105, 106, and 107/TOM BAKOWSKY, Photo/Graphic Associates II, Mississauga, Ontario; Pages 65 and 117/ JUNE ROESSLEIN INTERIORS, St. Louis, Missouri.

"We have to re-learn how to look at and choose colors. Colors should not be judged on their own, but must be viewed in combination. Only then can you see the true potential of a color."

Leslie Harrington

CONTENTS

Section III: Painting Projects and Techniques

FOREWORD

Every day, we are surrounded by color — blue skies, green grass, pink roses, yellow taxis, red stop signs and more. Because our world is filled with so much color, there is a tendency to take it for granted and give it little thought. It is often only when we are faced with a decorating decision or find ourselves contemplating the purchase of a new outfit for our wardrobes that we realize a solid decision, *based on color choice*, is required.

For many people, this is when indecision sets in. But it needn't, if you have an understanding of color, what it is and how it works. Armed with a collection of useful facts, you will begin to feel confident about your choices.

Where better to get information about color than from Benjamin Moore & Co. Limited — a family-owned paint company, based in Canada and the U.S., that was founded in 1883 by Benjamin Moore and his brother, Robert Moore. The company's philosophy is based on three "I"s: *Industry*, *Integrity* and *Intelligence*, a credo that has underlined Benjamin Moore's rise to become one of the top leaders in the paint industry.

This book aims to provide basic information to help you develop confidence in your color choices. It also gives you a short background of color trends and color associations, tells you how to decorate with color and illustrates inventive ways to use standard paint products that will provide your surroundings with a bright new look.

As a reference book covering all aspects of color, COLOR — A STROKE OF BRILLIANCE should answer all the questions you have had in the past, and any that might arise in the future. By the time you've finished reading it, you should feel comfortable with color and confident in your abilities to make informed decisions for your home.

COLOR TIDBIT

Which is the correct spelling: color or colour?

Color is the preferred spelling in the U.S.A.; in Britain, it is colour. In Canada, both spellings are acceptable — so Canadians can decide for themselves how they want to spell this colorful/colourful word!

LEARNING ABOUT COLOR

In learning about color we begin to understand more about an intrinsic component of our day-to-day lives because, more than anything else, color is information. In this section, you'll learn the basics of color theory, how you respond to color, color trends and much more.

What is color?

In scientific terms, color is light, which is carried on wavelengths that the eye absorbs and the brain converts into messages so that we "see colors."

Color is also information. It helps to distinguish flowers, birds, fish and animals. It can signal fear, anger and embarrassment. It tells us to stop at red lights and to proceed when the light is green. Color identifies ripe fruit or decaying vegetables and other foods.

How do we see color?

It is pigment that gives color to objects. Pigments have the ability to absorb some colors and to reflect others. An object that appears blue actually absorbs all of the other colors but blue light. The unabsorbed light is reflected back to the eye and the brain interprets the object as blue.

Two of the components that make up the eye are rods and cones; the rods permit night vision or vision in dim lighting. The cones — and there are three types of these — permit colored vision: *receptor I* picks up on the blue end of the spectrum, *II* on the green areas and *III* on the red end. Other colors are combinations of these three color areas.

Can everyone see color?

Almost everyone can see color. People commonly described as being "color blind" can actually "see" color, but they confuse hues that most people distinguish clearly. There are three types of color blindness: *protanope* (the most common), in which people confuse red and orange with yellow and green, *deuteranope*, in which people exhibit the same symptoms but are also unable to distinguish gray from purple, and *tritanope*, in which people confuse green with blue, and gray with violet and/or yellow.

Some diseases, alcohol and nicotine excess, and the aging process may also inhibit accurate color perception. For instance, the lens of the eye naturally yellows with age and this alters color perception. While there is no cure for inherited color blindness, color vision may be restored if an illness is cured.

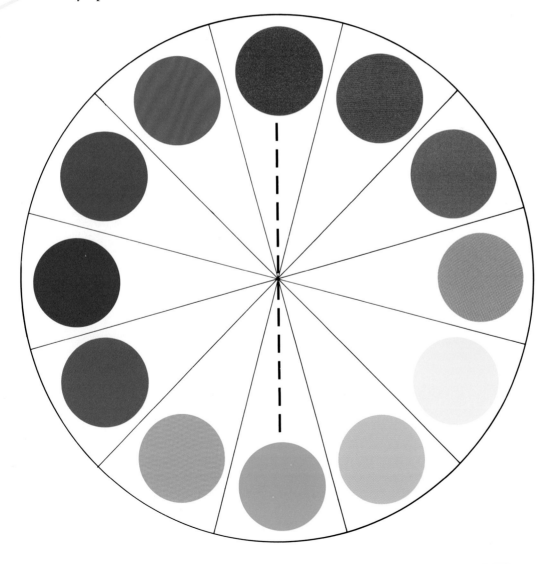

Glossary of Terms

A brief glossary of terms will make the understanding of color much easier.

Spectrum

When white light or daylight is passed through a prism, it will separate into color bands or a spectrum. This rainbow effect ranges through red, orange, yellow, green, blue, indigo and violet, red being the longest wavelength and violet the shortest wavelength.

Primary Colors

These colors are true unto themselves and cannot be made using any combination of colors. Primary colors are responsible for making all other colors. The primary colors of PIGMENT are blue/cyan (a blue tending to green color), red/magenta (a red tending to purple color) and yellow. The primary colors of LIGHT are blue, red and green, so be sure that you don't confuse these three colors with the primary colors of PIGMENT: blue, red and yellow.

Secondary Colors

The combination of two primary colors produces secondary colors. On the color wheel, secondary colors are located between the primary colors. They are orange (made of red and yellow), green (made of blue and yellow), and purple (made of blue and red). A true secondary color is made of equal parts of each primary color. Variations on this ratio will vary the hue of the secondary color.

Tertiary Colors

The combination of a primary and a secondary color in equal parts produces a tertiary color. The name of the new color is a combination of the two color names, for example, yellow with green produces yellow-green.

Color Families

All colors can be grouped into color families. These families represent the area of colors that have been used to make another color. There are six basic color families and they are represented on the color wheel: red, blue, yellow, green, purple and orange. A color such as pink would be from the red color family.

Neutral

Gray, white or black, without any identifiable hue or lacking color, are known as neutral or achromatic colors. Neutral colors, such as white and beige, characteristically match well with other colors. Neutralizing a color refers to lessening the effect of a specific color by combining it with its complementary color.

The following three terms are used

to describe color: hue, value *and* intensity.

Hue
This is another name for color and refers to the color family, such as red, blue or yellow. Even if a hue is tinted with white or shaded with black, it is still the same hue.

Value
All colors have what is known as high value or low value. In simple terms, this means that the lighter the color the higher the value, the darker the color, the lower the value. Value is the relative lightness or darkness of a color. The word "relative" is important because the value of a color depends on its neighboring color. For instance, two identical gray-colored squares will look different if one is placed against a white background and one is placed against

a black background. The gray will look lighter or higher in value on the black and darker or lower in value on the white. (The gray square will also appear larger on the black and smaller on the white

background. The same optical confusions are present with every color because every color has a value.)

Intensity
Intensity (or chroma, as it is sometimes called) refers to the brightness or dullness of a color and describes the degree of color strength. The more pure the color (i.e., the less gray), the higher the intensity. Red on the color wheel has maximum intensity. Bubble Gum Pink is a bright, high intensity color; Dusty Rose is a low intensity color. The brightness of a color can be altered by its choice of neighbor. If red is placed next to green, the red will look stronger against green than against another color because they are complementary colors. In decorating, colors with strong intensities are best used as accents—to provide sharp contrast and to add sparkle and life to a room.

Color Theory

The color wheel (see diagram on page 15) is an arrangement of colors in a circle in order of the spectrum. If the two ends of the visual spectrum are brought together, they will form a circle, which represents the color wheel.

The color wheel graphically places related colors close to each other and complementary colors directly opposite. The most common wheel has 12 colors. It is important to remember that the color wheel function is not so much to represent paint colors as it is to identify color families. This is useful when room decoration is being discussed, because proper color families, as well as tints and shades within those families, may be selected in harmony according to established decorating principles. The colors on the color wheel are known as primary, secondary and tertiary colors. Paint-color systems such as those found in paint-store displays, work on the same principles, with each paint strip representing one color and different values of that color.

Color Balance

Each color has its own level of strength. There are only two colors that have an equal weight: red and green. If primary blue and primary yellow are seen together in equal amounts, they will not appear balanced since the blue, which is deeper, visually appears larger and heavier than yellow ever can. Consequently a larger area of yellow would be required to balance a smaller blue area. The visual weight of a color can be altered by its value: lighter colors will visually appear lighter in weight than darker colors. Because of this, a balance between yellow and blue can also be achieved by using a deep yellow and a light blue.

Harmonious Color Contrasts

Complementary Colors

This is the name given to colors that are opposite each other on the color wheel. When complementary colors are viewed next to each other, they will intensify each other: the red appears "redder" and the green "greener." When complementary colors are mixed together

---

>

Complementary colors need not be boldly garish for them to work together effectively. The green walls — subdued though they are — make the red carpet really shine as an important decorating element. Without the green, the carpet would be far less exciting. The red cushion and paisley throw over the arm of the sofa likewise complement the green walls, thus the name for complementary color schemes! Note, too, how the red tones in the dining room chairs come alive against the green backdrop — all woods have colors which are influenced by their surroundings.

COLOR TIDBIT

Snow blindness

Long, continued exposure to very bright light can cause a temporary abnormality of the color sense in which all objects are tinged with red. It happens most frequently on Arctic explorations, on glaciers, in telescopic observations of the sun or in watching welding operations.

<

Triad color schemes – where three colors that are located equi-distant from each other on the color wheel are used together – always provide high impact. Usually, the first reaction to the notion of red, yellow and blue is limited to their use in children's rooms. However, this room shows how sophisticated and elegant these three primary colors can look when they are combined. One trick is to make sure that one of the colors is predominant and that the other two colors play supporting roles.

A second trick is to alter the value and intensity of the hues, thus using pale yellow as the predominant color, and graying-off the blue and red.

Soft yellow, yellow and yellow-green, used in this sitting room, show the dramatic effects possible when analogous colors are combined. The three colors, which adjoin each other on the color wheel, result in a soft, easy-living environment when used together. The fact that all three colors are of equal value further contributes to the overall softness, because no one color stands out from the other two.

V

in the right proportions, they will neutralize each other, or "gray" each other out. Complementary colors are red and green, blue and orange, and yellow and purple. In decorating, complementary color schemes are exciting and stimulating.

Triad

This is a contrast of any three hues on the color wheel that are located equidistant from each other. The most common triad color scheme is the use of the primary colors, red yellow and blue. This information is useful when considering colors for interior decorating.

Analogous or Adjoining Colors

This is a favorable color relationship that is created by the use of adjoining hues, which are called analogous colors. For example, in decorating, if you like the color yellow, you could combine yellow, yellow-green and green. This color harmony is a non-contrasting color scheme, which is soft and invites easy living.

Monochromatic Colors

This is a scheme based on one color. Tints and shades of one color can produce an interesting effect. In decorating, for example, a floor covering can be dark brown, the walls antique white and the draperies in a tan tone which can either be solid or contain a pattern. If an accent color is desired, the color family directly opposite brown, which is in the red-orange family, would be best.

"Warm" and "Cool" Colors

When looking at the color wheel, draw an imaginary line from north to south. On the east side of the wheel, you will see the warm colors. These colors are also referred to as "advancing colors." On the west side of the wheel, you will see the cool or "receding colors." These colors are not absolutes, however, for almost every color can be cool or warm, depending on what color it is compared to. If red is compared to yellow, red is the cooler of the two. If leaf green (with a yellow cast) is compared to sea green (with a blue cast), the blue-cast green is "cooler" than the yellow-cast green. If you are decorating and need to use a cool color, but want to decorate with red, be sure to choose a blue-cast red rather than an orange-cast red. Remember any color can be made cooler by adding blue. Use the color wheel for reference. Even though reds, oranges and yellows are commonly known as warm colors, all colors can have a warm side. To make a color warmer add yellow or red.

Chevreul's Laws

The hue, value and intensity of colors change depending on their neighbors. This fact, known as Chevreul's Laws, in recognition of the 19th-century French chemist who made many startling color discoveries, has applications for interior decorating. Consider these points:

- Light colors appear more striking against black or dark colors.

- All colors appear more striking against white or light colors.

- When dark colors are set against light colors, they look darker than they do on dark colors.

- When light colors are set against dark colors, they look lighter than they do on light colors.

- When two colors are placed next to one another, each tints its neighbor with its own complement. For example, complementary colors viewed side by side seem more intense than if viewed separately.

<

Since a monochromatic color scheme relies totally on one hue, great importance is placed on changing the value and intensity of that color. The hue here is red: a light-value red (pink) used in the tub chairs and accent cushions and a deep value red (burgundy) used for the sectional sofa. Neutrals play an important supporting role in monochromatic color schemes: here the neutral is gray, which appears in the carpeting and tables, and allows the eye to focus on the interesting part of the room — the furniture. (With the lush views of greenery seen from the panoramic windows, this room, in the daytime, is really an example of a complementary color scheme. By night, however, when the outside is in darkness, the real monochromatic color-scheme effects are most apparent.)

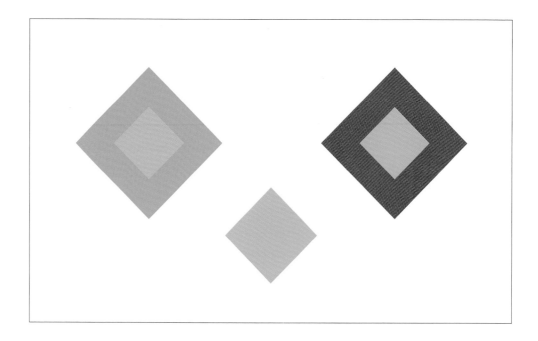

(see illustration above)

COLOR TIDBITS

Do dark colors really make a room look smaller?

No. It is a contrast of dark versus light colors that makes a room appear smaller than it really is. In order to keep a room looking as large as possible, eliminate contrasts in the values of the colors in the room.

Re-shaping a room with colors

There is an old myth that says if you have a long and narrow room, you can make it appear shorter and wider if you paint the end walls a dark color. This only works if you can see both ends of the room at the same time.

Going bold

If you want to try something colorfully bold, introduce it in small amounts first. That way you will eliminate the potential for costly mistakes requiring you to do the job over again in another color.

• Dark hues on a dark ground, not complementary, will seem weaker than if seen on a dark complementary color.

• Light hues on a light ground, not complementary, will seem weaker than if seen on a light complementary color. (see illustration above)

• A bright color against a dull color of the same hue, will appear duller than if viewed against a dull complementary color.

• When a bright color is used against a dull color, the contrast will be stronger when the latter is complementary.

• Light colors on light grounds can be greatly strengthened if bound by narrow bands of black or dark complementary colors.

• Dark colors on dark grounds can be greatly strengthened if bound by narrow bands of white or light complementary colors.

Color and Light

Without light there would be no color. And light — in its many manifestations — affects color. Most people are familiar with the traditional advice to use a warm color in northern-exposed rooms to make them feel warmer, since the north light tends to be "cooler" than that coming from the south.

Most people are also aware that colors will appear different when viewed under different light sources. The most common comparison made to illustrate this is in incandescent and fluorescent lighting. Generally, incandescent light will enhance warm colors and weaken cool colors, while fluorescent light tends to enhance cool colors and weaken warm colors. Because fluorescent lighting is economical to use, especially in commercial environments, the industry has developed numerous types of fluorescent lamps, ranging from cool to warm and even "full spectrum" lighting, which attempts to replicate natural daylight.

Natural Light

The most evenly balanced light is daylight, having almost equal parts of all the colors of the spectrum. Daylight, however, is never constant and will change at least four times a day: sunrise, high noon, afternoon and dusk. The light from the north tends to be the coolest, and because it has strength without glare, it is the one preferred by artists when selecting studio space.

Artificial light

Candle light — The warmest of all lights, candle light enhances reds, oranges and yellows. Similarly cool colors, such as blue and green, become dull and lifeless in candle light.

Incandescent — It has color-enhancing qualities similar to candle light, but because of its strong qualities, it appears whiter. It lacks colors from the blue end of the spectrum, and because of this, gives a poor appearance to cool colors.

Fluorescent — This is the lamp most often used in commercial areas and areas of the home where good overall lighting is required. Although there are many different types of fluorescent lamps, the one most commonly used lacks the warm colors of the spectrum. Fluorescent lamps tend to enhance blues and greens, and render reds, oranges and yellows duller. If using fluorescent lamps in the home, choose "full spectrum" or daylight varieties, which will enhance all the colors of the spectrum.

Halogen — Also known as quartz lamps, halogens are a special type of incandescent lamp, but the quality of light is much better than from standard incandescent lamps. The halogen lamp is more energy efficient and has a longer life than the standard incandescent. This lamp is becoming more popular in homes because it provides quality incandescent-type lighting in very compact units.

Mixing Colors

Color Mixing

All colors but red, yellow and blue are achieved by mixing variations of these three hues.

Pure colors mixed with white, gray or black suffer a deterioration of hue, which becomes pale, opaque, or dull respectively, causing the resulting color to appear weaker. Colors mixed with other hues, become "unsaturated," suffering a loss of color strength or intensity. The most unsaturated colors are those created by mixing complementary colors.

Additive Color Mixing

When two or more distinctive colors of LIGHT are combined to produce new colors, the process is known as additive color mixing. It's what makes colored television possible. Dots of light, in the three additive primary colors — red, green and blue — are blended by the eye, which consequently sees the full color spectrum. When the three primary colors of light — red, blue and green — are combined, they produce white light.

Subtractive Color Mixing

When pigments in paint, dye and ink colors are mixed together, they subtract qualities from one another to create a new color pigment. If paints or inks in all the three primary colors are mixed together, the result will be black *pigment,* unlike additive colors which would produce white *light.*

Tints, Shades and Tones

These are three commonly used terms. A *tint* is the addition of white to any hue; a *shade* is the addition of black to any hue. *Tone* is a term used to refer to a tint or shade. It is used descriptively, such as "a tone of blue or blue toned

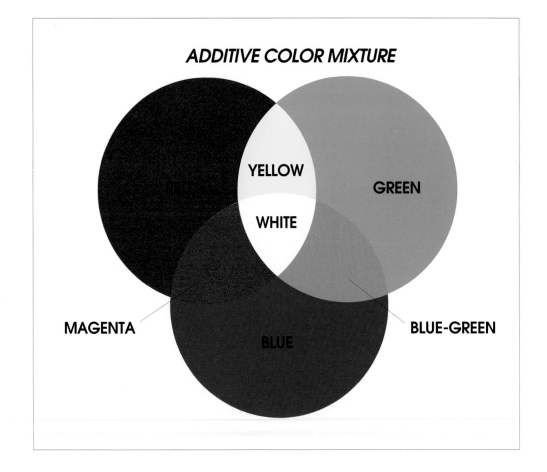

ADDITIVE COLOR MIXTURE

YELLOW

GREEN

WHITE

MAGENTA

BLUE

BLUE-GREEN

with green." Both rose and burgundy are tones of red; peach is a tone of orange.

Tones can also be achieved by using complementary colors. In the case of the color yellow, for instance, it can be made progressively darker or grayer by adding quantities of purple. The result of this procedure is the creation of a tone of yellow, and is sometimes referred to as "graying off" or "grayed color."

Afterimage

Afterimages are ghosts of colors that appear when the eye has been fatigued. Focusing for as little as ten seconds on a colored area such as a red spot will

fatigue that part of the eye's retina which is sensitive to red, causing a shift of sensitivity to its complementary color. Thus, a pale green spot — the complementary colored negative afterimage — will appear for a short time when one looks at a blank white surface. The afterimage of yellow is violet and the afterimage of orange is blue. However, if instead of looking at a white field, one views a dark or black field after focusing on a red spot, a positive image — or a pale red dot — will be seen.

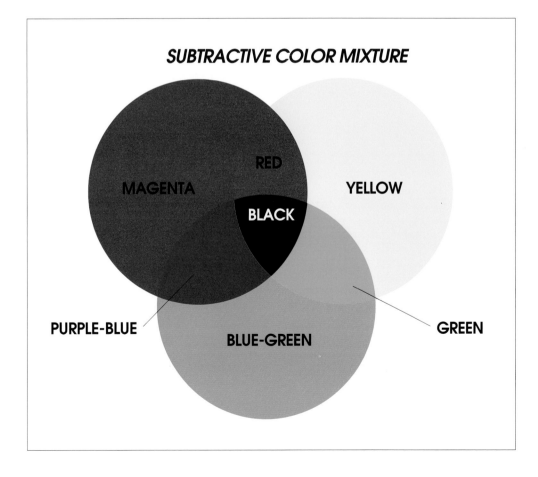

SUBTRACTIVE COLOR MIXTURE

MAGENTA

RED

YELLOW

BLACK

PURPLE-BLUE

BLUE-GREEN

GREEN

Color - The Silent Language

All colors affect us in two ways: we all experience a *behavioral response* to color, which is automatic and inherited and unaffected by sex, age, income, culture or environment and secondly, a *learned response*, which does depend on sex, age, income level, cultural background, environment and so on.

A behavioral response happens naturally without a person being aware of it. For instance, when a person sees the color red, the perception heightens (or elevates) blood pressure and causes sensations of excitement and heat. Another behavioral response to red is one of wanting to "reach out and touch." Everyone loves to touch red objects.

By contrast, consider this learned response to the color red: "stop, do not enter, danger." This response is learned from the use of red in everyday life in stop signs and stop lights. These are some of the first symbols we teach our children.

As people mature, they experience events, objects or images and develop special color associations with them. Because these associations are so personal, they may not be common to other people and this may result in a natural disagreement on color preferences. For instance, as a child you may have had a blue bedroom that you disliked and had to live with, so now, you feel negatively about that color. It is very common for people who work in hospital environments to have a strong dislike for green and they will therefore not use it in their homes.

The behavioral and learned responses of several colors are fascinating. Many of the following examples are taken from western civilization but as the world continues its cross-cultural growth, many of the associations from other cultures such as China, Japan, Russia, and so on, will begin to meld with the associations of the western hemisphere.

Remember that in looking at these colors, it is the true hue that is being discussed. Lighter and darker variations will alter the response slightly.

Red

Behaviorally, red stimulates appetite and energy levels, raises blood pressure and makes a person feel hot. It is the first color the eye sees in the morning and the first color to which a child relates . A "touch-me" color, it is frequently used for buttons and knobs to command attention. Red is often associated with square or cube shapes (that's why red-checkered tablecloths are so popular), passion, and spicy foods.

A highly emotional color evocative of love and lust and associated with everything from impulsiveness and courage to revolution, rage and anger, red appears in many old sayings: seeing red, red-blooded, red alert, red-light district, caught red-handed, red-letter days, red-tape, roll out the red carpet, scarlet woman.

It was the Egyptians who began the tradition of "red-letter days." It was their custom to begin new paragraphs with a red letter and to emphasize the total of a series of numbers in

>

Because red stimulates appetite, it is a favorite color for dining rooms. While red often appears garish in daylight, by night light, it tones down and mellows into a warm, rich neutral background color. Red also stimulates conversation — a plus in any social setting.

red ink. Accountants use red ink to make debits in ledger books — hence the concept of being "in the red." The term "red tape" arose from the historic practice of binding legal documents with just that — red tape. Nowadays, the term is associated with bureaucratic regulations and obstructions.

Pink

Associated with things sweet, pink is a favored color for packaging candy. It is also associated with the sweetness and innocence of young females and thus a favorite color for little girls' bedrooms and clothing. Pink, known to have short-term calming effects, is often the color of walls in prison holding cells.

V

Pink is a favorite color for bathrooms because of its positive reflective qualities on the skin. This warm color makes everyone look as though they had a healthy glow. The warm qualities of pink will be enhanced under incandescent lighting rather than with fluorescent lighting.

The color conjures up images of pink elephants, being tickled pink and in the pink.

Orange

Associated with exuberance, joviality, vigor and boldness, orange seems to suffer from an identity crisis! No one is ever "orange with envy," "orange with rage," or "feeling orange." Orange is always a hot color; unlike red and yellow, it cannot be cooled down. One of the strongest associations with this color is thirst, which is why orange pop always looks so much more refreshing than a cola drink.

The behavioral responses to orange are gregariousness, activity and joviality.

V

Yellow is a favorite color in hallways for numerous reasons. First, it is a difficult color to be surrounded by for long periods of time; hallways tend to be spaces that people merely pass through without spending much time in them. You get a short-burst positive reinforcement of the color without being dragged down by long-term viewing. Secondly, because hallways tend to be devoid of natural daylight, and yellow has such a strong psychological association to sunshine, it helps to bring the sense of sunlight inside.

Yellow

The most difficult color for the eye to process and see, yellow is the least popular hue on the spectrum. Behaviorally, yellow stimulates memory. That is why legal notepads and reminder notes are yellow. It reflects poorly on the skin and often makes people look as though they are suffering from jaundice. Bright, bold, strong yellow is associated with "value-for-money"; it is the color of choice for generic packaging in supermarkets. Yellow is identified with enlightenment, gold and sunshine — but don't paint your house bright yellow! Studies show that this will decrease its value — an understandable conclusion when you remember that it is the least favorite color.

The color yellow is identified with high-pitched sounds, sour smells, heat, speed and the shapes of triangles and pyramids.

Yellow suggests detachment, anticipation and a philosophical attitude. It is often associated with cowardice. Think of the phrase, "yellow bellied" or a "yellow dog" — used to describe a person who crosses a picket line during an industrial strike.

Green

Instinctively, green evokes a sense of relaxation, comfort and quietness. It is an undemanding color, very "middle-of-the-road," neither too hot nor too cold.

The easiest color for the eye to see, and therefore the most restful of all the colors, green is the color of concentration and relaxation. The neutral of nature, it is associated with spring, new growth and new beginnings.

The smell of the outdoors, fresh scents and rounded triangular shapes are associated with the color green.

Who hasn't at some time been green with envy, green around the gills, longing for some greenbacks (money)? Because it is such a restful color, "green rooms" are provided in theaters and television studios for actors to wait until they are to perform in front of the lights.

Blue

Variations of blue are the most popular of all the colors. Physically, blue will help to lower blood pressure on first view. Non-threatening, it is known as the color of trust, as in true blue, longevity and dependability. People who enjoy being alone choose blue for its sense of coolness. Considered a neutral color, you can live with it forever.

Blue suggests salty tastes, a compensation for sweet and musty smells, and is associated with circle shapes.

Blue appears frequently in phrases: once-in-a-blue moon, blue funk, crying the blues, blue ribbon, blue blood.

Purple

Behaviorally, this color can also help to lower blood pressure, suppress appetite, quell internal dialogue and calm overactive glands. This is not only a

>

Because green is the color of concentration and relaxation and is the easiest color for the eye to focus on for long periods of time, it is the perfect choice for a den, study or bedroom. The darker the green, the more relaxing and mellow the room will feel.

hard color to figure out because it exhibits characteristics of both red and blue, it is a difficult color to live with for long periods.

Purple's strongest associations are towards floral scents, royalty and religion. Oval or free-form shapes best represent the spirit of this color.

Who doesn't occasionally enjoy purple prose? And think of the honor to have been bestowed with the purple heart for bravery. The color violet — its less-intense relative — suggests romance and imagination.

Black

The color of non-commitment, this is an "easy-out" color. Considered neutral, it has traditionally been associated with death and mourning, although now it is a sophisticated and elegant

V

Because blue is the color most able to induce calming effects, it is the perfect choice for children's bedrooms. The fact that blue is associated with dependability and trust aids in creating a sense of security for the child.

color. Black suggests dignity, power, worldliness, aloofness, intimidation and mystery.

The negative connotations of black are many: blackmail, blackballed, black listed, black sheep, the black market. But the concept of "black tie" suggests sophistication and elegance.

White

A color suggestive of purity and innocence, it conjures up images of naiveté, youth and cleanliness.

But like its opposite — black — white is a color of many negative connotations. Think white lies, white

---

▼

A high-fashion color, purple injects strong impact and style in a formal drawing room. A combination of blue and red, the purple walls, here, bridge the red carpeting and blue draperies and upholstery fabric. Other colors such as yellow or pale blue could have been used on the walls, but it is purple that gives that extra punch and glamour.

elephants, whitewash (to cover up an embarrassing fact), raising the white flag of surrender.

Brown

Traditionally associated with warmth and comfort, brown speaks of solidity, reliability and the comforts of home. It is a color with strong and positive food associations: brown eggs, brown bread, brown rice, brown sugar. Brown comes from the orange family and elicits similar, although less intense, behavioral responses.

>

Nothing beats white in a kitchen! Because a kitchen contains so many elements, white on the walls gives the room a unified appearance in coordination with the white cabinets, counters and appliances. In some rooms, white can be almost too sterile looking, but a kitchen can never look too clean.

V

Black in this kitchen dining area, makes the walls invisible as it acts as a neutral color that supports and enhances everything else in the room.

Traditionally, black is used in furniture, not on walls, but here, the reverse is true, showing how black on the walls can give a room a dramatic appearance.

V

No color suggests hominess better than brown! In this case, the color comes from the wood tones, which further enhance the warm characteristics traditionally exhibited by this color. Brown's strong positive associations with food make it a good color choice for any eating area.

Gray

Gray suffers a lack of assertiveness so it suggests confusion as in "gray area." But it also is associated with intelligence, as in the glib phrase, "gray matter," referring to the brain.

Gray traditionally indicates guarded behavior, as well as a sense of discipline, and deliberate or planned actions.

A bland, albeit sophisticated color at times, there is a particular shade of gray with very positive connotations: silver. Think silver lining, born with a silver spoon in the mouth and that glamorous symbol of Hollywood: the silver screen.

Color Associations and How They Evolve

Much of the following information has been adapted from COLOR COMPENDIUM *by Augustine Hope and Margaret Walch.*

An ability to respond to color is present soon after birth. The first color a child sees and relates to is red. This is a behavioral response. The favorite toys of young children are usually red. (Is there a lot of fighting among your children over certain toys? Eliminate the red ones and see if there is a difference in their behavior.) Studies show that young children cry more when they are in rooms painted yellow because yellow is the most difficult color for the eye to see. Adults can leave a yellow room when they tire of being in it, but babies cannot.

From the age of two onwards, color becomes one of the strongest influences in a child's life. Counsellors use color when helping troubled children adjust to the demands of society; the colors for which a child shows preference offer clues to his or her emotional life. When vocabulary skills are not yet developed, color provides important clues to a child's well-being.

For instance, under the age of four, children who show a preference for "warm" colors such as red, orange and yellow tend to be sympathetic, dependent on others for affection,

COLOR TIDBITS

Why are flamingos pink?
The natural color of flamingos is white. They turn pink because they eat carotenoid-rich crustaceans such as crab, lobster, shrimp and crayfish. The red, orange and purple pigments prevalent in these crustaceans color the feathers and skin of the flamingos which eat them.

Is a "blue moon" really blue?
Alas, no. The phrase a "blue moon" refers to the rare occurrence when a second full moon occurs within a calendar month.

How do chameleons change color?
The basic green color of chameleons is due to a combination of several factors. The skin of the chameleon is made up of three layers, each a different color. The first layer contains yellow carotenoid pigment. The cells of the middle layer are blue. The third layer contains brown melanin. The chameleon controls its color through various nervous reactions, which trigger the various layers to become stronger or weaker. When the animal is in a "normal" state, the three colors combine to produce a green color.

Blue Chip
Usually used in reference to preferred stocks and safe investments on the stock exchange, the term is derived from the highly-valued blue chips used in the game of poker.

White House
Much is made of the fact that the president of the United States of America lives in the White House. In fact, its gray, smoke-tarnished walls were painted white after the nation's capitol was burned by the British in 1814.

COLOR TIDBITS

What color is Taupe?

One of today's most popular neutrals, and the most unknown color, it is a combination of beige and gray. But since there are more than 500 variations of beige and gray, there are even more variations of taupe.

At dawn and sunset, why does daylight tend to appear reddish?

The mixture of colored wavelengths are not always consistent during all times of the day. In the morning or at night, there is a lack of blue-green light, thus resulting in the red fire glow of a sunrise or sunset. On cloudy days, daylight usually has less red and orange, resulting in a drab day.

White elephant

Why is a hard-to-get-rid-of item sometimes referred to as a white elephant? It started with a long-ago King of Siam who used to make gifts of white elephants to countries he wished to ruin by the cost of the animals' upkeep.

Remembering color

We have all tried, but it is harder than we think, to carry a color in one's "mind's eye." It is said that we remember colors for only two to three seconds. The moral of this story? Take color samples to the store when trying to match colors.

cooperative and well adjusted. Children in that same age range, who tend to favor "cool" colors such as blue and green, are described as intellectually inclined, selfish, determined and "loners."

The child who uses black in his paintings may be exhibiting signs of a troubled state. Red used freely indicates an uninhibited love of life, whereas if it is painted violently, it may reveal either hostility or a desire for affection. Excessive use of blue may indicate a controlled anxiety. A new brother or sister in a household often results in the older sibling painting in blue. Lots of yellow indicates a happy, carefree child. Green suggests self restraint, self sufficiency, self confidence and emotional well-being. Purple is the least-used color among children — except at Easter time in cultures where that occasion is celebrated.

By the time children have reached their teens, all their learned responses to color will have accumulated and these will be constant throughout the rest of their lives. Color preferences and responses change in adulthood only in reaction to major life changes, such as moving to a new country, or cultural, global and environmental impacts.

Color Coding

Color coding is an integral part of our normal world. It distinguishes animals

> The gray walls in this bedroom show how this color traditionally lacks assertiveness — a positive factor because it means that the architectural details and furnishings take center stage. A great neutral background color, gray is the best bet for showing off special accents.

COLOR TIDBITS

How do iridescent colors come to be?

The iridescent colors apparent in birds' feathers, flies' wings and soap bubbles come not from the color of the objects themselves, but from light rays which are, themselves, colorless, striking these objects.

What makes a rainbow?

Rainbows are created when the sun's rays are reflected and refracted by the falling raindrops during a shower. The size of the raindrops determines the intensity of the rainbow: the larger the drops, the brighter the colors of the rainbow. Very brightly colored rainbows are produced by intense showers of large uniform-sized raindrops.

Flags and Colors

There is a strong relationship between the geographic location of a country and the colors of its national flag. In northern-hemisphere countries, red is the predominant color; in southern hemisphere countries, green predominates. The colors selected for flags are also chosen for their instinctive qualities. For instance red, white and blue are favorite flag colors, the red signifying courage, white for virtue and blue for wisdom and truth. A nation's population tends to have strong positive associations with the colors of their national flags. For instance, Italians will choose reds and greens over other colors, while French, British and American citizens prefer red, white and blue, and Germans tend to like reds and yellows. Many companies with headquarters in these countries have capitalized on these associations such as IKEA (a Swedish company) and Air Canada in Canada.

(a white polar bear, a red fox), birds (a blue jay, a red-headed woodpecker), and flowers (a red rose, a yellow daffodil).

Color connects the viewer with an object more quickly than any other identifying characteristic. For this reason, color is much used as a simple code to signify complicated concepts or systems. The simpler the code the better it is for a smooth-functioning society. That is why the color red is universally used to mean STOP — it is understood by any age, culture or educational background.

Think of the telephone book. Almost everyone in western countries understands the difference between the white pages, yellow pages and blue pages and can instantly flip to the appropriate section when desiring specific information.

There are color-specific international codes for roads, traffic and industry.

On roads and traffic:
Green: information
Blue: hospitals and quiet areas
Yellow: danger, caution
Orange: work areas
Red: do not enter, stop, danger

In industry:
Yellow or black stripes: beware of stumbling
Red: fire protection
Orange: dangerous machine parts which can cut, crush, burn or cause shocks
Green: safety
Blue: equipment is under repair, do not move or use without permission
Purple: hazardous nuclear energy
Yellow: physical hazards such as projections

Color and Food

Color has a very great influence on our choice of foods, consequently food producers ensure that their foods are the correct flavor, ripeness — and color.

Brown is associated with cereals, breads and well-cooked meats. One of the biggest problems that microwave manufacturers had in the past was convincing consumers to cook meat in them because the cooked meat never looked "brown" and therefore ready to eat, even though it was.

White is found in foods such as rice and bread, which often contains refined or processed flour and sugar. Dairy products such as ice cream are lightly colored to suggest sweetness.

When margarine was first introduced, it was colored yellow because white margarine would not sell. The shade of red in tomatoes often dictates the price and the speed with which they will sell. Peas in the can are usually dyed so they look more appealing.

In packaging, the best color is the one that represents the food itself. Brown beer bottles enhance the amber color of the beer. Green and yellow works well on canned corn, attracting us to the natural taste and quality of content.

The Importance of Color Names

The names of colors are, for the most part, only marketing terms applied to colors to aid in their acceptance and to promote the sale of products. But names can make or break a color's acceptance — and success.

Descriptive names such as Bubble Gum Pink and Candy Apple Red evoke strong color pictures. Some color names will last a long time while others will change as influences do. For example, Tobacco Brown of the 1960s and '70s has been renamed because smoking has been found to be a hazardous habit. Also, Chalk White — a traditionally popular color — was seen to be losing its favored ground as the message of a "clean environment" became the goal. Once the color was given a cleaner name — China White — it soon returned to near the top of the popular colors list. By 1971 Ivory, also a popular color of long standing, was perceived as growing old, and paint sales in this color slipped. When its name was evocatively changed to Oriental Silk a decade later, it once more rose to the top where it has remained.

Color History

The history of color through the centuries is a topic of utmost fascination and interest — as the multitude of books written on this subject proves. Anyone wanting to know how cave dwellers produced colors from plants and stones or what the traditional colors of the Victorian period were — and everything in between — would enjoy reading books on art history or color theory, such as HISTORY OF MODERN ART by H. H. Arnason.

COLOR TIDBITS

Why do apples look riper on the tree than in your hand?

When complementary colors are viewed next to each other, they tend to enhance each other's color quality. Red and green are complementary colors, so when the red apple is seen hanging amid the green leaves of the tree, the green makes the red look redder and the red makes the green look greener.

Why are peaches packed in purple paper cups?

The purple enhances the unripe color of the peaches, making them appear more "appetizing" and riper. Peach producers use this technique to encourage consumers to buy their product even though they're not quite ripe and ready for eating.

Why do butchers display their meat trays divided by rows of plastic grass?

Even though enlightened consumers know that the redness in meat – beef, in particular – is not necessarily a mark of quality or freshness, they still prefer to buy beef that is bright red in color. What color will make red look its reddest? Green, of course, being its complementary color. The green "grass" dividers so beloved by butchers are there to enhance the color of the meat.

Color Trends in the Twentieth Century

It is an accepted fact that the use of color is a "trendy" concept. In the twentieth century, color tendencies and directions in clothing and furnishings have identified themselves as cyclical, oscillating with the changing attitudes and economic circumstances of each decade.

The 1920s, for instance, was a decade dominated by two opposing design influences: Art Deco and the Bauhaus. The color direction of Art Deco design swept the spectrum and was characterized by emerald green, Indian coral, black, red and polished chrome. The Bauhaus style, on the other hand, emphasized the use of natural materials, and embraced white as the dominant color.

One other influence at play during this decade emerged in mid- and southwest America, reflecting the influence of architect Frank Lloyd Wright and his Prairie School Style, which was characterized by reddish-brown and ocher.

In the 1930s, bright colors were introduced to the masses and color-coordination became a pre-occupation for both designers and consumers.

The 1940s, being taken up with wartime, were relatively drab and colorless, but in the 1950s, the introduction of many new technologies and the development of plastics resulted in an explosion of color. This was the decade in which the first Universal Color Systems were introduced to the paint market, providing consumers with custom-mixed paints, and widely expanding the possibilities from 50 colors to 1000.

In 1951, Forest Green was the most popular paint color according to Benjamin Moore's archive files. A deep rich green, it is still in favor today. In 1953, Willow Green moved up to top the list and it stayed there for four years, beating out the ever popular white shades. By 1975, this color had declined in popularity so drastically, it was dropped from Benjamin Moore's line of ready-mixed paints.

In the 1960s, color television came into millions of homes but it is the next decade that is most colorfully memorable. Remember the psychedelic '70s? That was when color was expressed in music, clothing and graphics. Empire Gold, a color that had been around for many years, reached its peak popularity just as the decade was opening but a dozen years later, it had disappeared, never to return.

By the 1980s, color had become such an obviously integral part of life that it was impossible to go anywhere without seeing color in everything.

Now, in the 1990s, colors seem to be developing as much less saturated. A new sun-drenched, bleached-out, worn look to colors is coming back. White and black will continue to be strong, but not in their pure form. There will be many different deep shades of black. There will be an overall yellowing, i.e. warming, of the palette, which is nature-inspired. Green is expected to dominate, ranging from yellow-greens to rich bronzed greens and some tinged with silver.

Decision Makers

In industry, products are manufactured with the help of designers and colorists, who know that a consumer's decision to purchase any product is based about 60 percent on its color. Obviously, the right color can "make or break" a product and determine its success or failure as a manufactured product.

Colorists look to many areas for help before making decisions on new colors for their products: the competition, related products, past color successes and failures, global influences, economic conditions etc.

Does the Past Influence the Future?

There is a school of thought that maintains if you keep anything long enough, it will come back in style again. This is partly true but when something does become fashionable again, it is usually sufficiently different to make the original not quite "right" in the new context. If a color comes back into popularity, chances are that the other colors with which it is teamed are new and different and that its original base has been slightly altered, giving it a new appearance. For instance, the green of the early '80s was blue-based, in the late '80s, it was yellow-based.

COLOR TIDBIT

What's in a name?

Professionals in the color business prefer to discuss colors using a numerical notation system. Most people, however, like to have a name attached to a color because it allows them to visualize the color in their mind. Successful color names allow one to immediately recognize the color without even seeing it, such as Candy Apple Red, or Sky Blue.

In the early 1990s, the color Avocado came back in favor, but not paired with Harvest Gold the way it was in the '70s when it was last popular. Avocado in the '90s is teamed with red, violet or purple — unthinkable combinations twenty years ago! And it has been given a new *90's* name: Guacamole — that trendy dip for veggies and corn chips whose primary ingredient is avocado, and whose name conjures up exciting thoughts of the southwest and its influences — a popular trend into which this color fits perfectly, thus ensuring its successful return.

Color Cycles

Color cycles — a term to describe the shift of color popularity — last about seven years. In fashion, you may see color cycles changing more quickly but in the home, seven to ten years is a common cycle, since practically, it is not economical to change color more often. When purchasing an expensive item, which is expected to have a long life, the consumer would be wise to make sure it is of a classic color, because these have a very long color cycle. Not all colors will have the same color cycle; bright strong colors will have shorter life spans than classics such as navy blue, and black and white, which can be timeless.

COLOR TIDBITS

Fad

A color with only a short term of popularity in the marketplace, fads usually have a lifespan of six months to a year.

Trend

The popularity of a color that lasts longer than a fad, possibly as long as six years or more. While trends have been known to develop out of fads, this is rare. Trends are usually based on issues that affect everybody, such as environmental concerns, politics, technology, globalization, and so on.

DECORATING WITH COLOR
Answering Questions/ Getting it Right

Many people need help in making color decisions; they find the process too complicated and problematic. Asking ourselves a series of questions will usually help to solve our color problems.

The trick is knowing the "right" questions to ask. If you have ever asked for advice from people who are experienced in color, you've no doubt noticed that they first ask you many questions before supplying an answer or solution.

Here are some questions to ask yourself to help make color choices:

What is your lifestyle:
Do you like to entertain?
Do you like to travel?
Are you "stay-at-homes"?

If you lead a busy life, your decorating colors should be durable—colors that do not show dirt and general wear-and-tear. White, cream and ivory are not durable colors; navy blue, black and brown are.

How many children do you have and how old are they? (Include grandchildren and all the little ones in your life.) If there are often lots of children in your home, it's a good idea to avoid light colors and pale shades.

>

Using light colors against dark is one of the best ways to accent objects. Here, there is a layering effect at play: the dark walls enhance the lighter pine cabinet, which in turn, enhances the white upholstered chair, which — because it is the lightest object in the room — is the piece the eye sees first. This is a good object lesson for one of the most important decorating principles: establish first the feature element, then layer colors to support it.

Previous page:
An excellent example of how the colors in the draperies were pulled together in the sponged wall treatment. See Benjamin Moore's FANTASY FINISHES booklet or video for how-to's.

What are your favorite activities, sports and hobbies?

Every activity has color associations, and you will find that you will react favorably to colors that are associated with the activities you like — green and golf, blue and flying, white and skiing, etc.

What types of lighting do you have, or prefer:

incandescent, fluorescent, halogen, candles?

Assess the following rooms:

The living room:
- do you watch TV?
- do you gather around a fireplace?
- do you entertain here?

The dining room:
- how often is it used?
- is it only a "showpiece"?

The bedroom:
- do you watch TV?
- is there a fireplace?
- is there a desk area?
- do you like to read in bed?
- is the room used in daytime or only at night?

The bathroom:
- how many people use it?
- is it used for make-up?
- is it small or large?

The kitchen:
- what is your cooking style?
- how many meals are prepared per day?
- do you entertain?
- do you eat meals there? do the kids?
- what are the adjoining areas?

The family room:
- do you watch TV here?
- do you listen to the stereo?
- how many people use it?

- what other activities happen here?
- do you eat in this room?

Assess the room contents:
- What objects must stay in each of the rooms you want to decorate? Make a note of each item and its color, gathering together a sample or swatch of each, if possible. If it is not possible to have samples, get paint chips that match the colors of items you cannot get samples for. This way, you will have a conveniently transportable file to use for reference
- What objects do you hope to change, or want to add to the room immediately? Make a list.
- What objects will you be replacing or purchasing in the next two years? Make a list, but there is no need to choose colors yet. You should merely have these things in mind.
- What is the most expensive item to be replaced or purchased? This will be your starting point.
- List all the items you want to change in order of approximate cost. Paint should be last, because in most cases it is the least expensive.

Once you have the answers to these questions, you are ready to start.

Search the stores for colors, patterns and textures, starting with the most expensive item you need and working your way through your list to the least expensive. But, don't actually buy anything yet — just collect samples

>

The combination of black and white always produces maximum emphasis and drama. Because the eye is first attracted by the lightest detail, the wood trim in the room is enhanced to the extreme because of the black walls.

of colors and fabrics, adding them to the samples of existing objects that you gathered earlier. Choose more than one color, because as you start choos-

V

For least emphasis, use tone-on-tone colors. It is the shape of the objects and the textures of the fabrics that give this room interest.

ing other colors you will find that some color families are going to look better together than others. Here is a hint — make sure that one item has pattern in it. It could be a fabric or wallpaper, but remember this general rule: the more expensive the item the less pattern it should have.

Decide on what you want to be noticed first in a room: the art? sofa? carpet? Your walls should be near the

bottom of the list. They are meant to be a foil or background for all the other things in the room. The lightest and brightest color should be used on the items to be focused on the most. Less focused areas should be duller and deeper such as walls, wall-to-wall carpeting etc.

The color of every component in a room is important, so consider each of these aspects:

- *Ceiling* —stippled, drywall, acoustic tile
- *Walls* — paint, wallpaper, mirrors, ceramic tiles
- *Trim* — painted, natural wood
- *Floor*—carpet, ceramic, hardwood, lino, tiles
- *Furniture* — sofa, chairs, dressers, tables, desks, book shelves
- *Fixtures* — kitchen and bath cabinets, appliances, toilet, tub, sink
- *Counters*— stone, laminate, glass, metal
- *Decorative accessories*

Keep in mind the following helpful hints and basic concepts in decorating a room:

- Use light colors against dark for accent — light-colored objects will be noticed first; the supporting objects should be darker. This does not necessarily mean black and white, but some contrast.
- For more emphasis and the most impact, use light and dark with complementary colors. For less emphasis, use light and dark in the same color family.
- For maximum emphasis, use white and black.
- For least emphasis, use white with ivory, cream or beige.
- If you tend to eat most meals on casual furniture rather than formally at a table, choose patterned fabric — it will show less spills and spots.
- If you wear shoes in the house hardwood floors may wear better than carpet, and they are easier to keep clean.
- In small areas, paint the walls and trim in a light, cool color which tends to make the room appear larger.
- In larger areas, paint the walls in a medium-dark color, which tends to make the walls advance, thus providing the illusion of shrinking the room size.
- In long, narrow rooms, where you can see the two end walls at the same time, paint the opposite, smaller walls with a dark color, which tends to "pull" the two walls together. In square rooms, paint one wall (preferably the one that is seen on entering) a different color to provide interest.
- For color flow, link the rooms with color to create a feeling of spaciousness. For example, the dining room is often connected to the living room, so both should be painted in related colors of the same hue. To continue this theme of spaciousness, the same floor covering should be used in both rooms.
- Camouflage design defects by painting them the same color as the adjoining wall surface.
- For balance and proportion, in order to minimize a "cut-up" appearance to any room, avoid using contrasting colors for wainscotting and upper walls. For example, when painting a bathroom, it is recommended that shades in the same hue as the ceramic tile be used on the walls and ceiling when possible.
- Painting two adjoining walls one color and the other two remaining walls in a different color will create an unbalanced room. The only time it is

recommended that two adjoining walls be painted a different color is when you want to balance an unbalanced room such as in the case of a fireplace in one corner, which appears heavy and disproportionate.

• Consider the exposures: it is preferable to use warm colors in rooms that face north and east, because they are generally considered to be "cold" rooms and often exposed to a minimum amount of direct sunlight. In rooms that face south or west, it is

Light walls/dark trim and dark walls/light trim are both valid decorating techniques. The big decision is which is the best combination to use. These two photographs show both and in both cases, one of the main elements in the rooms is reflected in the trim color. In the room on the left, the white background of the carpet and upholstery is repeated in the trim. In the room on the right, it is the green of the sofa that is matched perfectly on the trim. If the color of the furniture had been used on the walls, the furniture would have become "invisible."

V   **>**

preferable to use cool decorating colors because the rooms are considered to be warm, being exposed to extended periods of direct sunlight.

Selecting the Right Colors for the Right Room

This information is meant only as a guide, since there is really no right or wrong choice, but some choices will be better than others. If colors other than those suggested are desired, they can be used as accents or in smaller amounts.

Remember the right color for you is going to depend on your personal activities, family preferences and current style trends. Many of these assumptions are based on information contained in the first section of this book, which describes human response to colors and associations. Use this information as a guide only. Rules can be broken!

Kitchen

Watch out for red in the kitchen be-

cause it stimulates your appetite! Better kitchen colors are blue, because it

has cool, refreshing, non-food related qualities; green, because it is related to natural food and health; yellow, which is sunny, bright, clean, and associated with a lemon-fresh scent; and white, which is clean and fresh, and great for appliances, although too much of it can make a room look sterile.

V

The colors in the living room upholstery fabric reappear in the rooms beyond, showing the unifying effects of color flow from one room to the next.

Bedroom

Bright, sunny yellow can be a difficult color to live with in large amounts over a long period of time, so use it with care. Golden yellows, on the other hand, are easier to live with — think of the morning glow at sunrise. Green is a good bedroom color because it is associated with concentration and relaxation. Blue and purple are also relaxing — and sophisticated. And don't forget about pinks and peaches — they're stimulating, warm, friendly and inviting.

Den/Study

Beware of black because it can be very depressing, and too much white can be boring and hard on the eyes. Yellow feels fine — briefly — but may become overwhelming over longer periods. The best choices are green, for concentration, light blue if you spend long periods of time in this room and any colors in the red family if you use computers all day long because of afterimage effects. (see page 27)

Living room

Any of the "warm" colors are inviting and stimulate conversation, but stay away from dark grays, unless teamed with lots of bright and light colors.

Dining room

Red is the best — and the darker the better! Gold is great, too, and black creates a terrific dramatic effect. Blues, however, tend to look depressing under low lighting levels, while white is too stark for that intimate feeling.

Bathroom

Pink and peach give good reflective qualities on the skin, but yellow produces just the opposite. Grays are depressing without other colors, and white is excellent, particularly for fixtures, because it looks clean and sterile, exactly the properties you want in a bathroom.

Selecting the Right Colors for Fixtures and Furnishings

Carpet

Taupe and gray — and any other neutral shade as long as it is not too light — and rich, deep greens are the best carpet colors. Light blue can be "iffy" so stay away from it if you are not sure. Black shows every mark, thread and speck of dust and red should only be used if you really love it. White should be avoided if you have children or pets.

Appliances

Your best bets are white, black, almond or a color that matches the kitchen cabinets. Any other color should not be considered.

Furniture

Hunter Green looks expensive, navy blue is a timeless traditional and cream, taupe and other neutrals are always good bets. Black can be too heavy and difficult to work with unless you are willing to have dark walls for balance.

Bathroom Fixtures

White is the all-time favorite choice because it "reads" clean. Cream or ivory are also popular. Bear in mind that dark colors, which look great in the showroom or store, are less successful in the home, because they must be continually cleaned, since soap residues show so clearly.

Draperies and Blinds

Choose colors that are not too trendy and use accent colors only on side panels and toppers, unless you can

(continued on page 60)

Guidelines for "Exterior Decorating"

by Kenneth X. Charbonneau,
Color and Merchandising Manager,
Benjamin Moore & Co.

Consider these hints for successful exterior color combinations:

• Be aware of the roof color. It is an item that most homeowners are not going to change until absolutely necessary. Don't try to ignore the color, work with it to create a tasteful color scheme.

• Take natural materials on the house into consideration — brick colors, stone, slate, even concrete. Select colors that will enhance these surfaces.

• Even the landscaping and terrain should be noted.

• Use 4 or more colors:

    1. Body or siding color.

    2. Trim color.

    3. Accent color — usually on shutters.

    4. "Punch" color — usually on front door. Define the front door, as the entrance or "introduction" to the house. Punch color can also be used on the mullions of windows.

• Be kind to your neighbors — be aware of neighbors to your left or right. It is merely courtesy to consider how your house colors and theirs will reflect on the streetscape itself.

• Utilize manufacturers' color cards. Most major paint manufacturers have taken care in laying out the colors in suggested combinations.

• Remember colors intensify and look brighter in daylight on the outside of a house than they do on the color card in the store.

• Color preferences are going lighter. Gone are the heavy browns, earth-tones and murkey greens. Light- to medium-value colors are emerging.

• Soft contrast in color combinations are "in," with tone-on-tone trim and house body colors replacing the once-popular light-body, dark-trim combination. The use of soft-contrast color combinations results in the house appearing larger.

(continued from page 57)
afford to change your window coverings often. Match them with the wall color, unless it is very trendy, in which case, match them with the trim, especially if it is cream or white. Consider matching the window coverings with other expensive items such as the sofa, accent chair, or carpet, since they will likely be replaced at the same time.

Ceramic Tiles
Neutrals are the best. Light colors are even better. Nothing beats white, or matching your fixture colors.

For kitchens and bathrooms, blues are by far the favorite for wall tiles and a good easy living color. Green is a second choice.

For floors, any natural colors from terra-cotta, beige, taupe, white, gray, blue and green.

Cabinets
Dark colors should be used on cabinets only if you have a well-lit room, otherwise choose light colored woods, or white or almond and make all the cabinets throughout the house the same, especially if it is small.

Counters
Because dark colors have poor reflective qualities, solids tend to show marks easier and white shows stains, your best counter-top choices are lighter midtones, stone textures, grays and beiges with texture.

The Most Frequently Asked Questions

There is a familiarity to the questions that get asked most often about colors and their use in home decor; obviously, many people share the same concerns. The following sampling could well answer questions that y o u ' r e wanting and waiting to ask.

Q *1. Why do colors appear so different on the color chips from on the walls?*

A While there are many reasons for this, let's look at some of the factors at work here. Knowing about them will help you to make correct color choices in the future. The main reason why colors appear different on the chips and on the walls is because of the colors that surround your choice color on the chip. Whenever you look at paint chips in the paint store, notice that they are usually displayed amidst other colors, against a white background and under fluorescent lighting. Any color that is viewed against something white will appear darker than if it is seen against any other color. When selecting colors, be sure to eliminate any white surrounding color.

Because colors will affect one another, view your color options against the other colors that are to be used in your room and not against the colors in the paint store. Remember that complementary colors such as red and green, blue and orange, or yellow and purple will intensify each other when viewed together.

The size of the color chip can itself often create problems. It is very difficult for most people to visualize an eight-by-ten-foot wall from a one-by-two-inch piece of paper. Fortunately, larger paint chips are now available in most paint stores. To imagine the paint chip as a wall, hold it between your fingers, eliminating all other colors and squint your eyes. Still, because there is such a larger area of paint on the wall, remember it will appear significantly more intense. Choosing a color one shade lighter will not always eliminate this situation, but choosing a color that is the same value but not as bright (i.e. grayer in tone which should be selected from the neighboring paint chip strip) will help.

Sheen will also certainly affect the value of a color. The more glossy or shiny a color is, the deeper it will appear.

Color is likewise affected by the light in which it is viewed. Lighting

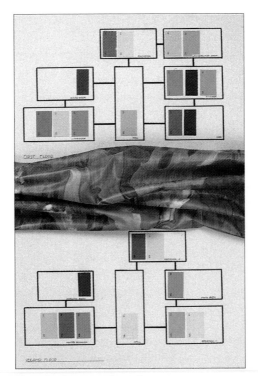

Developing a color scheme.
(see questions 4 and 5)

from incandescent bulbs tends to enhance the warm tones in a color. Fluorescent lighting will enhance the cooler tones in a color. Be sure to take your color samples home and view them in the room in which they are to be used, under the lighting conditions that will be the most prevalent. For example, if you use your dining room mostly at night and use candles for lighting, don't make your color choices during the day by natural light.

Q *2. Why does the color of paint in the can look lighter than when it dries on my walls? How can I be sure I am buying the right color?*

A In most cases, wet paint in the can will be a little lighter than when it dries on the wall. To ensure that the color you are buying matches the color chip of your choice, put a little of the paint on a piece of non-absorbent white paper and allow it to dry. In 99 percent of all cases, it will match. This, however, does not eliminate the problem of imagining what the paint-chip color will look like on the wall. Never judge a wet paint color, whether it be in the can or on the wall. Colors change during the drying process. When using deep or clean colors, ensure that a deep base primer is applied first, as this helps to develop the color. If you try to save time and money by skipping this step, you'll be disappointed with the results. Only judge a color after the entire area is painted and the walls have dried.

Q *3. I bought a pink paint for my living room but when I got home, the color was brighter than I thought. Is it possible to change the color to make it less bright or do I have to start all over again?*

A Yes, you can change the color of your paint. Pink is one of the hardest colors to choose. Quite often it will look too bright and need *dulling down*. Depending on how bright your pink is, you will want to take it back to the store and ask them to add a touch of green. The green — the opposite color to red — will aid in neutralizing the red and therefore change the brightness. It is important to understand that there is no point in adding black or white because these will just change the value lightness or darkness of the color.

Q *4. Where do I start when developing a color scheme?*

A A successful color scheme uses a minimum of three colors together. If you have more confidence, you might consider using more colors to a maximum of six, but remember, the more colors you use, the more difficult it is to achieve success in decorating.

How do you arrive at the three basic colors? Take inspiration from an existing pattern already in your room

— in the window coverings, upholstery fabrics, cushions, etc. If there is no pattern already in the room, then your first job is to introduce one. Pick a pattern whose colors you like, one which contains some of the colors already found in the room's carpet, window coverings, etc. Identify three color families in the pattern: the main color, the secondary color and the third, which will act as the accent color.

When determining color placement, you must first consider the main focus of the room. If you have chosen your colors from a sofa pattern and you use the predominant color of the pattern as your main wall color, the sofa will become less apparent. It is wise to select the secondary color for your walls if you want to maintain the sofa as a focus. Consider, too, that your eye is attracted to the lightest color in a room first. So, if your walls are *not* the first thing you want to be noticed, do not paint them the lightest color. If you are concerned about dark colors making a room look smaller, refer to question 7. The main color does not have to be the lightest or the background color in the pattern. It will, however, be the most prevalent color you'll use in your room. If you choose as your main color, the dominant color in the pattern, then you will probably lose some of the emphasis and impact of that pattern in the room.

The secondary color will not be used as much as the main choice, but may appear as a piece of furniture or a carpet. The function of this color is to provide visual interest, variety and balance.

The third color — the accent color — is commonly thought of as the brightest or darkest color in the pattern. It is the color that will be used the

least. Since it is used so sparingly, a strong color tends to make a good accent color. It is contrast that makes for a great accent. White, then, can be an accent color, especially if the room in which it is applied tends to utilize darker colors. In most cases, successful accents are those that are complementary to the main color.

Once these colors are established, you can place them in the room to produce the effect you want: light colors against dark colors for emphasis, cool colors against warm for strength and contrast. The most neutral color in the room should be used on the largest and most unchangeable items such as carpets, window coverings and major furniture pieces.

Remember, within the three colors you have chosen, you can expand your range by combining different values of the same color, for example, light and dark blue.

Q *5. I am building a new house. How do I begin to choose my colors?*

A There are myriad things to consider, complicated by many factors such as one's inability to get into the new

>

Color is an important part of the "new" look in this room. It may be hard to tell, but many of the old elements are present in the new room. The colors in the new upholstery fabric on the old furniture (now painted white), establish the color scheme which is repeated in the custom carpet and on the walls. Interior design: June Roesslein Interiors, St. Louis, Missouri. (see question 4)

house under construction to make your color selections under true-to-life lighting conditions. As well, you can only visualize colors against one another from small color-chip samples. And you must take into consideration, the color preferences of other people who will also be living in the house.

When starting a project of this magnitude, it may be wise to consult a professional. You can still do the work yourself, but if you find you get stuck and need an unbiased opinion, you will be glad to have a professional's advice.

To start, make a list of all the "fixed" elements in your house that have to be considered, such as bathroom and kitchen cabinets, counter tops, hard flooring, etc. These will be the first color decisions you'll have to make. If possible, keep these as simple as possible: the fewer the color changes in these major fixed elements, the more color options you'll have open to you throughout the house.

Now that you have these major decisions out of the way, you can start to have fun with color. Study the check list for each room, determining all existing furnishings, the use and function of each room. Establish a main color palette for the entire house, using something you treasure as your primary focus. It might be a favorite painting, patterned scarf — anything to which you can refer when you think you have strayed from your established palette and may be getting lost!

Once the main palette is established, look at individual areas (groups of rooms that have related functions) such as the dining room and kitchen, or the bedroom and its adjoining bath and closets. Once again, select a pattern and choose three colors from it to establish a palette for the area, starting with the most expensive item (window coverings, carpet etc.). Choose your main color. It will likely be the most neutral of the three colors because you'll want it to last for the longest length of time — unless you think you'll be able to afford to change the drapes or carpets after a few years when you're tired of them. Then move on to selecting your secondary color and third accent color.

Q *6. What colors will go together and look good together?*

A The first part of the question can be answered by saying that any color goes with any color. Having said that, however, it should be said that generally, warm-cool color combinations, such as green and rose work best, but rose can be used with peach as well. Keep in mind that most colors are either blue-based or yellow-based, so greater harmony will be achieved if you combine colors of the same base.

The second part of the question is a little more difficult to answer because "what looks good together" is obviously a very personal preference. The key to getting colors that look good together is harmony, balance and interest. Usually, one color is more predominant than the others, in terms of the amount used; one is strong and is usually used more sparingly. The best

rule of thumb is to look for patterns with colors already combined: in a scarf, picture, piece of fabric or wallpaper.

Choose three or four colors from the pattern and use them as the basis for your color scheme. Don't prejudge a color individually; see it as part of a group. If you do not like one of the colors in your selected pattern, do not discard it for this reason, simply use it in small amounts for accent. This color is needed for the combination to work successfully.

Q 7. Do light colors make a room look larger?

A If everything in the room is a light color, the room will look larger. It is not necessarily the color of a room that determines its perceived size, but rather the contrasts in color values. To keep a room looking as large as possible, use colors that are similar in value — that is, all light colors or all dark colors.

Q 8. Are beige, brown, off-white and gray the only "neutral" colors?

A Any color can be a neutral color, but these colors are neutral by definition. That is one of the great things about color. In general, a "neutral" is the color used most prevalently in a color scheme. In some countries — Russia and Peru, for example — red is considered a "neutral" color. In nature, green is the "neutral" or background color for all other colors. Consider your own wardrobe: is dark blue your personal "neutral"? Think about your favorite pair of blue jeans — just about any color gets paired with them!

For a color other than beige, brown, off-white or gray to be a successful "neutral," it should be a color of a deep value, and not too bright.

Q 9. I am looking for a true white. How do I know if a white is really white?

A This is a tricky question, for what really is white? Since all colors will appear different, depending on their neighbors, true white will be the one that looks the whitest when compared to other whites. Surprisingly, white in the paint industry is still a tinted color, because it does not occur naturally and must be made. Therefore, the quality of the paint will, in some cases, dictate the cleanliness of the white. Titanium Dioxide is the main pigment used to make most things white, from plastic to paint. In lower-grade products, less Titanium Dioxide means less white. To ensure that you are getting the whitest white possible, buy only top quality products and compare them to the whitest thing you can find. But be

realistic: in paint, you may not find a white that is as bright as in a quality paper.

Q *10. My husband prefers very light walls, because he says it will make the rooms look larger. I, however, would like to use some color on the walls, especially something darker than off-white. How can I convince him that this is a good idea?*

A This is a very common question but ask your husband and yourself this: what is wrong with some rooms looking a little more cozy? If it is a family room, living room, bedroom, or dining room, they are usually more inviting if they are cozy looking. But did you know that it is possible to use darker colors and still achieve a large feeling? Just think about the way we distinguish a room size: by its corners. How do we see corners? By shadows. If a wall is painted light — not dark — which color are you most likely to see shadows on? The light color. So if the dark color hides the shadows, it will allow for the walls to open onto one another and therefore make the room appear larger.

Remember, too, that more than color it is contrast that makes a space appear smaller. If you already possess many light-colored objects that you will continue to use in this room then it would be wise to keep the walls light,

but they do not have to be the lightest color in the room. When you walk into a room your eye is attracted to the lightest thing first. In most cases, our walls are the lightest areas, because we are trying to keep the space as large as possible, but they are rarely the first thing we want to see.

Q *11. All my walls and woodwork were painted white five years ago, and, at the time, looked great. However, today, the woodwork looks a different color from the walls. Why?*

A Traditionally, walls are painted using a latex paint, while baseboards, doors, etc., are painted using alkyd or oil-base paints for greater durability. The natural color of the oil resin, the base component of all oil-base paint, is yellowish. In latex products, the base is mostly water and therefore does not have this yellow quality. Although manufacturers try very hard to keep latex and oils similar in color, over time, the oil products will yellow more than

---

>

Kitchen cabinets are the perfect spot to cut loose with paint colors. Just be sure to prepare the surface properly before beginning to paint. Top and bottom cupboards need not be the same color. Here, the white uppers keep a small kitchen looking spanking clean and bright, while the dark lowers will show spots and dirt less. (see question 15)

the latex. Like most things, the better the quality of the product, the slower this process will develop, but it is still inevitable. So, if you do not want to have to paint every three or four years, paint your walls and trim in the same product, either latex or oil. Remember, the higher the sheen, the more durable the finish, so if you elect to use latex, use eggshell finish on the walls, and satin or semi-gloss for the trim, where you require more durability.

Q *12. I like the look of colored ceilings but I do not know where to stop. How many differently colored ceilings can one house have? Also, is it possible to paint stippled ceilings? Will darker ceilings make my rooms smaller?*

A Colored ceilings are great but you do have to consider where the color is going to stop. Look for a natural place, where a room ends, at an overhead arch, etc., but if this does not exist, then the color will have to be carried into the next room until a natural stop occurs.

How many colors are an excess depends on other factors in the rooms. For instance, one house that received rave reviews, had all the walls painted in a traditional three-inch tone-on-tone cream stripe (see "Striped Wall Finish" on page 90 for directions), and all the trim and crown moldings were accented in white. Every room had a ceiling in a different color: one red, one

blue, one hunter green and one gold, and tying it all together were area carpets the same colors as the ceilings. Why did this work so well? The home had small, individual rooms, which allowed for a natural stop of each color. The walls were very neutral and not the focus of the room. The designer had successfully reversed the traditional roles of room colors in which the unifying light color is placed on the ceilings and the color is placed on the walls. This may not be exactly what you are looking for, but it may inspire you.

Yes, it is possible to paint a stippled ceiling. If it has been painted before, use a latex flat paint and a high-pile roller. Remember that two light coats are better than one heavy coat so do not over-roll. If the ceiling has not been painted before, it is recommended that you use an oil-base paint, particularly if it is a newer home. In new construction, very little binder compound is mixed with the spray texture, so that when you get it wet with the latex paint, the water in the paint acts as a loosening agent and softens the stucco, resulting in a mess. By using oil the stucco remains intact and will not loosen.

To answer your question of whether a dark ceiling will make the room look smaller, I can assure you that in fact, the opposite will occur. Most people think that because the ceiling will seem lower, the room will decrease in size, when in fact the ceiling visually "comes down," pushing the walls out and increasing the perceived size. If possible, try wrapping the ceiling color onto the walls slightly and separate with crown moldings for a great visual effect.

There is one more point to consider: standard 7-foot-six-inch or 8-

foot ceilings are designed to feel comfortable in rooms in which you stand more often than you sit. How many rooms do you stand in more frequently than sit? Two: the kitchen and hallway. So it is alright if the ceiling feels a little lower; it will actually make you feel more comfortable.

Q *13. I have a blue-colored sofa, a beige-colored carpet and peach-colored drapes. What color should I paint my walls?*

A While it may be hard to accept, all colors go with each other. When deciding on the wall color, you must first establish what you want to accent: the sofa, the carpet or the drapes. Ideally, you should choose only one.

If you want to emphasize the drapes, the walls should be any color other than that of the peach-colored drapes. If you were to paint the walls peach, then the drapes would blend into them and not be noticeable. The best color to accent the peach is a deeper, complementary cooler color such as blue. The darker and stronger the blue, the more striking the drapes will appear.

If you prefer to emphasize the blue sofa, the same principles apply. A dramatically lighter or darker complementary and warm color will make the sofa appear fresh and new. That would suggest the walls be painted either a light or dark orange, peach or rose color. The ideal color would be one from the same color family as the drapes,

which will help blend the drapes into the walls. If you want the drapes to be noticed, use a peach that is the same color but either lighter or darker.

If you want to emphasize the carpet, consider this: the flooring, unless it is a piece of art, or a valuable carpet or extremely interesting, should never be the main feature in a room. It should be a neutral support for other pieces in the room such as the furniture. With a beige carpet, the wise course of action would be to try to make it appear "better" than it is by painting with darker colors, since they will make the carpet appear lighter. If lighter wall colors are desired, use contrasting lighter woodwork and moldings, which will bring out the slight color tinge.

Q *14. Should I use the same color of carpet throughout the entire house or can I change it in some rooms?*

A If you have a small house, keep the flooring colors and materials to a minimum; the fewer the changes, the larger your house will seem. However, if you have a large home, you can probably afford to make color and material changes.

In an open-concept house, it is difficult to change carpet colors because you see into many rooms from any location. But if you live in an older house, you probably have many separate rooms and this makes it easier to change flooring colors and materials without their being too noticeable. However, if you are considering re-sale value, the same color carpet throughout the house is the best choice.

════════════════════

Q *15. Can I paint my kitchen cupboards?*

A You can paint almost anything. First, remove all hardware, hinges and doors. Proper surface preparation is one of the most important steps in any painting project but nowhere is it as vital as in painting any kitchen-related surface. You must remove all dirt, grime and grease from the surfaces so that the new paint can adhere properly.

Wash with T.S.P. (trisodium phosphate) and rinse thoroughly. If the surface is especially slick and shiny, a light sanding will also be beneficial.

Then, prime the surfaces, using Benjamin Moore's Enamel Underbody. If you are starting with a dark-colored surface and repainting with a light-colored paint, use two coats of light-colored primer paint and one finish coat. Let each coat of paint dry thoroughly, then sand, before applying the next coat. If you are using a color that is dark, tint your primer close to the finish color. While oil-base paints are usually used for the finish coat, you can use latex paint as long as it has a gloss finish. The shinier the finish, the more durable the coating will be. Use high-gloss for a contemporary look or satin finish for a casual, country look.

When all the painted surfaces are

completely dry, re-install the hardware and doors. And don't forget that if you dislike the existing hardware, now is the perfect time to change it! Even the location of door handles and drawer pulls can be moved: simply fill the screw holes before painting and drill new ones after paint has dried.

════════════════════

Q *16. Can I paint over wallpaper or do I have to remove it first?*

A If the paper is securely attached to the wall, you may attempt to paint it, but wash it thoroughly first. It is also a good idea to prime it, especially if it is a solid vinyl paper. Use Benjamin Moore's Wall Grip #1 or Benjamin Moore's Enamel Underbody. Paint as you would any wall surface, but keep in mind that you will likely see the seams. For this reason, why not consider a decorative paint finish such as rag-rolling or sponging to help disguise the seams?

>

The paneling in this indoor garden room is reminiscent of the material used to fix up many basement areas. Its bright blue color freshens the paneling, which was washed with T.S.P. and painted with a coat of primer before the final color was applied. (see question 17)

Q *17. I have a very dark family room that I would like to make lighter. All the walls are covered in a very dark wood paneling. Can I paint it and will this help?*

A The answer to both of your questions is "yes." Painting paneling is very easy. Just think of it as a new substrate and follow the same procedure as for kitchen cupboards. (see question 15) Wash, to remove any wax, dirt or other foreign substances. Prime, using Benjamin Moore's Underbody (alkyd) or AquaGrip (latex) and allow to dry. Finish with any wall coating. For an interesting look, consider using a fantasy finish on your paneling, such as one of the many described in Benjamin Moore's booklet, FANTASY FINISHES. If you are concerned about seeing the grooves in the paneling, use a dragging finish, or don't worry — the grooves add interest, so any finish looks great.

Q *18. We have recently purchased an older home and would like to re-decorate, but at the same time, be sensitive to the period style of the home. Can you suggest historical colors or possible reference material?*

A If you are looking for historical color information, Benjamin Moore has a collection of 174 Historical Colors that have been researched by the Green Park Commission in the U.S. These colors are for interior and exterior use and reflect the tone and intensity of the colors that were popular during the 18th and 19th centuries in North America.

You might also like to consult reference books such as CENTURY OF COLOR — EXTERIOR DECORATION FOR AMERICAN BUILDINGS 1820-1920 by Roger Moss; VICTORIAN EXTERIOR DECORATION by Roger Moss and Gail Caskey Winkler; and HOW TO CREATE YOUR OWN PAINTED LADY by Elizabeth Romada and Michael Larsen. Also, many cities have historical councils that have guidelines or archives that you can use for source material.

Q *19. We are going to repaint the outside of our home. I would like to know what colors are best since we do not want to have to repaint again for a number of years. Also, on which areas of the house should we use the accent color?*

A Trends in exterior colors do not change as fast as in interiors. The best

>

Hardwood floors can be lightened and refinished using any color of stain. Light colored floors help to open up a space, giving it a larger and more spacious feeling. Don't stop at the floors when in a refinishing mode: do the trim, moldings and staircase, too, for a new look. (see question 21)

colors are neutral off-whites, beige, grays, camels, etc., for the main body of the house, since these are the most difficult areas to paint, requiring ladders or scaffolding. Most houses will require three or four colors to look really great. Obviously, the more detail there is on the exterior, the more room you will have for experimenting with color. Use a secondary color on the garage door and any unattractive detail such as the eaves. Save the "punch" (accent) color for the front door, since this is where you want to attract attention. The punch color can be bright and cheerful and not used anywhere else on the house. Use your gardens for influence. If you have lots of pink roses in front, then this could be your punch color. With new technology in computer color matching, you can actually take a flower petal to your local paint store and have the computer match the petal color to paint. Since the door is so easy to paint, don't be afraid to make a mistake.

One of the major shifts in exterior painting is a decrease in the use of contrasting trim. Newer homes are getting smaller, but since we would like them to appear larger, it is best to decrease the amount of contrast between body and trim colors.

Q *20. The outside of our house has stucco, vinyl siding and eavestrough, and metal railings. Is it possible to get the same color of paint for all these different surfaces?*

A Yes, the same finish coat can be used for all these surfaces, but the appropriate primer must be applied first. The stucco will likely not need priming, nor the vinyl siding and eaves, if Benjamin Moore's MoorGlo is used, because it is a self-priming product designed specifically for these surfaces. But any new or exposed areas should be primed, and galvanized metal should be primed with a galvanized metal primer.

The metal railing should be primed using a metal rust inhibitive primer, especially if there is any indication of rust on the surface, followed by the same finish coat as for the siding, unless you prefer a high-gloss finish, which can be mixed to the same color.

Q *21. We have an older home with hardwood floors we are planning to refinish. I like the new light-colored stains with a pickled look. Is it possible to lighten our floors and re-stain them using one of these new colors?*

A Refinishing hardwood floors is becoming more and more popular. If

> *Kitchens benefit from the use of innovative stains on cabinetry. Just like paint, stains come in 2000+ colors. Why not mix and match them for a really up-to-the-minute look? (see question 22)*

your floors are solid wood, there would be no problem sanding them down and refinishing them using any color of stain you desire. However, if the floors are just a veneer, you will not have much to sand before sanding the veneer off. In this case, you may choose to try to strip them and follow with a light sanding. Once your floors are stripped/sanded, hopefully most of the original color will have been removed. If the color of the floor is still darker than the finish stain you wish to use, then you may try a wood bleach to lighten the floor further. You can use a stain that is darker than the floor color, but it is difficult to go lighter, unless you use a heavily pigmented stain that will not let much of the wood grain show through. (When it comes to sanding the floor, it is wise to let a professional do the job, since it is not easy to control the sanding machine and you may get gullies or alleys in the floor.)

Q 22. I like all the new colored stains you see in magazines, but when I go to the paint store, I can never find these colors. Is there a special formula or secret that I don't know about?

A You should be looking for Benjamin Moore's Neutral Blender, which is a stain base before any pigment is added. This lets you add the color of your choice, selected from paint chips. The store will tint it for you just as they do paints. Remember that it may appear slightly different to what

you are expecting since the color is translucent until you spread it on the wood where the background color will affect the finished appearance. You may have to experiment a little.

Q 23. What is the difference between varnish, urethane and Varathane? Which coating is likely to yellow more?

A Urethane and Varathane are essentially the same product. Urethane is the generic name; Varathane is a trademark name for urethane. The difference between varnish and urethane is that urethane tends to be harder than varnish. If urethane is used on a coffee table, a hot mug will not leave a mark, whereas if a varnish were used, it might. Varnish tends not to yellow as much as urethane, which can be a benefit when using light pastel stains or no stain at all. Latex urethane or varnish will yellow least of all or not at all.

Q 24. I want to try ragging-off in my room using pink and green. Which color should I use first?

A A good general rule of thumb is to start with the color you want to see the least and end with the color you want to see the most. So start by establishing which will be the dominant color — the pink or the green? Because these two colors are complementary colors, they will tend to neutralize each other when layered on top of one another. So it would be wise to make one deeper or stronger than the other and again, the stronger one will be more predominant. If you want to see both colors equally, change your method of application to *ragging-on*. See instructions for "Ragging-On" on page 106.

Q 25. I have just become interested in refinishing wood. However, sometimes when I attempt to re-stain a piece I have just stripped, it becomes blotchy. How can I stop this from happening?

A This problem is not only limited to refinished wood. The reason you are experiencing a blotchy effect is because the wood is absorbing the stain at different rates. To even out the porosity of the wood, you must use a clear product that is similar to a primer for paint coatings, such as Benjamin Moore's Neutral Blender. It will allow the wood to continue to absorb stain after it has been applied. You might also encounter the same problem when working with soft woods such as pine, birch and whitewood. You may have noticed that when staining these woods, the stain tends to collect in the heavily grained areas. Neutral Blender will give

a more uniform appearance with new or re-finished woods. Always test on the underside of furniture or a spare piece of wood to see which looks the best.

Q 26. We just bought a house that has fabric vertical blinds on the windows. Can I paint them and what should I use?

A You can paint fabric vertical blinds. There is a remote possibility that it will not be successful, but chances are you'd throw them out anyway if you weren't able to change their color. Make sure they are clean and dust free. Use a latex flat paint, lay the blind on a flat hard surface and roll on a heavy coat of paint. Allow to dry, then turn over and paint the other side. Let dry before re-hanging. Be careful not to roll or fold blinds.

Q 27. Does the customer have any say in the colors coming into the marketplace?

A For a color to gain popularity, it has to be proven in the marketplace. Sales are therefore a good indicator of whether or not a color is going to be successful. If consumers dislike certain colors, they will not purchase products featuring it and the color will fail and quickly disappear from the market-place.

The general public has a say in forthcoming colors in indirect ways, too. Look at the current importance of the environment and the public's concern for it. This has sparked a major resurgence in colors related to land, water, sky, stones and other natural elements.

PAINTING PROJECTS AND TECHNIQUES
Getting Down to Work

Painting walls and trim using traditional methods is a fast and easy way to enliven and rejuvenate home decor. However, new products now available, make it possible to have even more interesting and intriguing color effects.

Take a look at these great ideas; they will add interest and charm to your home without costing a lot of money and without taking a lot of time to produce.

GRANITE FLOOR

This project is very simple, but will require a couple of hours on your knees — less time if you have a friend willing to help. The object is to make a concrete or plywood subfloor resemble granite.

Step #1: Paint floor white with latex floor paint. This is especially important if it is a basement floor, because there may be moisture present, which can cause oil-base paints to peel.

Step #2: After the paint is thoroughly dry, use a pencil (not a pen or marker as it will bleed through the paint) to draw a grid pattern on the floor. A four-foot by four-foot grid is recommended because the larger the grid the less work involved. However, in smaller

Previous page:
One of the basic glazing finishes — ragging-off — gives this bedroom a soft romantic look. See Benjamin Moore's FANTASY FINISHES booklet or video for how-to's.

>

Combining two techniques in a room can work well, as shown in this bedroom. Walls are ragged and the floor is sponge-painted to create the look of granite.

rooms such as kitchens and bathrooms, you may consider a smaller grid.

Step #3: Using one quarter-inch sign painters' tape, place the tape along one side of your pencil line. Do not place the tape on top of the lines.

Step #4: Now for the painting; one quart of latex flat paint in each of two colors will be enough to do most rooms. Pour the paints, one-quarter of an inch deep, into pie plates. Start in the corner of the room which is located the farthest from the door and work your way out of the room. Use one sponge for each color, alternating the

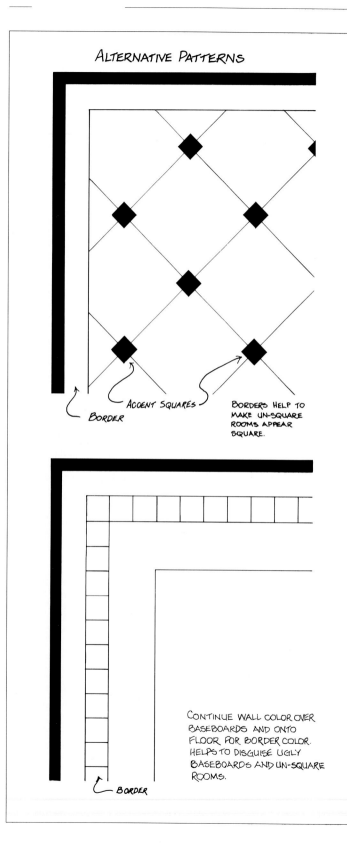

ALTERNATIVE PATTERNS

BORDER

ACCENT SQUARES

BORDERS HELP TO
MAKE UN-SQUARE
ROOMS APPEAR
SQUARE.

CONTINUE WALL COLOR OVER
BASEBOARDS AND ONTO
FLOOR FOR BORDER COLOR.
HELPS TO DISGUISE UGLY
BASEBOARDS AND UN-SQUARE
ROOMS.

BORDER

two colors so you don't have to wait for each color to dry.

Step #5: Remove tape as soon as you are finished painting.

Step #6: Finish with two or three coats of high-gloss clear floor varnish or urethane.

This project is also featured in Benjamin Moore's FANTASY FINISHES Video. You can make a faux granite floor take on more interesting detail with the addition of accent diamonds.

Simply add the pattern of six-inch squares drawn on the floor when you are drawing the original grid pattern. The accent squares are placed at the intersection point of each grid line. During the taping step, make sure you include the new squares by taping around them as well. The time required is not much more than you are already investing, but the rewards will be great. Paint the floor as specified, and when dry, return to the job and paint in your accent color in the accent squares only. The easiest way to do this is to cut a square the size you want out of a piece of newspaper and use the square hole as a stencil template to sponge on the color.

For color suggestions, keep the overall area of the floor neutral using gray (#1481) and beige (#1004). Use the accent color of the room in the diamonds (pink #1279). This way, when you change the accent color of your room, you will only have to re-paint the accent diamonds.

SLATE FLOOR

Creating a "slate" floor is similar to replicating a granite look and can be done on either concrete or plywood. Don't fill in all the imperfections, as they will add character to your final project. Be sure to apply caulking to the major seams in the plywood, so water will not seep under the floor.

Step #1: Paint the floor the base color, using Benjamin Moore's Latex Floor and Patio paint. Remember the color of the background will be the grout line color. You could use light gray for the background and a darker blue gray (#1651) over top.

Step #2: Using a pencil and a ruler, draw the grid pattern or trace around a piece of cardboard the size of your square.

Step #3: Using one-quarter-inch-wide sign painters' tape, mask off the grid design as for the granite floor.

Step #4: Only one square will be painted at a time. Mix glaze by combining approximately five parts Benjamin Moore's Glazing Liquid with one part Satin Impervo, which has been tinted

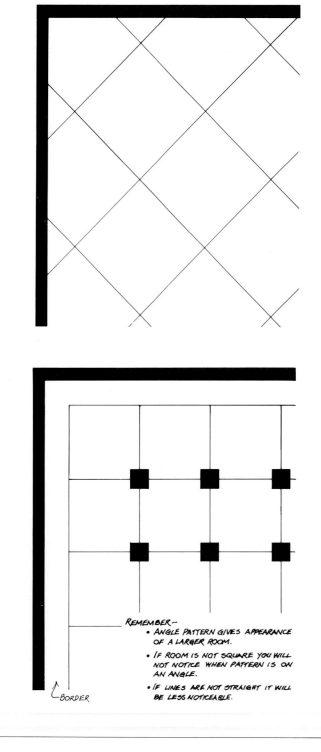

ALTERNATIVE PATTERNS

REMEMBER—
- ANGLE PATTERN GIVES APPEARANCE OF A LARGER ROOM.
- IF ROOM IS NOT SQUARE YOU WILL NOT NOTICE WHEN PATTERN IS ON AN ANGLE.
- IF LINES ARE NOT STRAIGHT IT WILL BE LESS NOTICEABLE.

BORDER

to the color that you want your glaze to be.

Step #5: Using a three-inch-wide roller, apply glaze to one square.

Step #6: Take a light-weight plastic drop sheet, similar to a dry cleaners bag, and cut it into rectangles six inches wider than the square size and three times longer. Accordion-pleat the plastic in your hands, and lay on the wet paint, lining up the lines of the plastic with one direction of the square.

Step #7: Smooth the plastic into the paint; leave on square until ready to reposition on next square.

Step #8: Continue to paint alternate squares and lay on the plastic in the same direction as the first square. Remove after pressing the plastic to the floor.

Step #9: After finishing every other square, stop and allow the floor to dry overnight. This way you can still use the room.

Step #10: Paint the remaining squares using the same method, but change the direction of the lines so they go in the opposite direction to the first ones. You will only need one piece of plastic for each day, because you can re-use it from square to square.

Step #11: Remove tape as soon as you are finished, and allow to dry overnight.

Step #12: Finish with two coats of high-gloss floor varnish or urethane.

STEP #3

STEP #5

STEP #7

STEP #10

STEP #11

ABSTRACT FLOOR

This is a very fast floor to create, and fun, too. It would be great in a family room, basement play room, or home office. The key to the success of this floor treatment is to find a shape that you can re-use. This effect also works well on canvas dropcloths to create your own area rugs.

Step #1: Paint the floor or canvas white using floor paint, or whatever background color you wish. This will be the color of your squares.

Step #2: Paint border color about six inches wide around the edge of the room or canvas.

Step #3: Use low-tack painters' tape to mask off another border three inches inside the first. This will leave a white (or your background color) band when removed.

Step #4: Randomly throw your shapes on the floor (canvas) in any pattern, using as many or as few as you desire.

Step #5: Using Benjamin Moore's Utilac spray paint in any color — randomly cover the areas where the shapes lay. You do not have to totally cover the entire floor as a solid; it looks more interesting if you don't. Make sure to open the windows whenever you spray paint and wear a face mask.

Step #6: When the paint is dry, remove the shapes and you'll find the pattern created beneath.

Step #7: Remove the remaining tape to reveal the white border.

Step #8: Varnish or paint the floor with urethane for durability.

STRIPED WALL FINISH

This is one of the simplest and most elegant finishes, producing a tone-on-tone striped wall. As a variation, slightly tinted colors on a white background can also be interesting and equally elegant.

Method One:
The Fast Way

Step #1: Paint walls in the color desired, using Benjamin Moore's Regal Wall Satin latex flat, not eggshell.

Step #2: Allow to dry for two days.

Step #3: Using a plumb line or level, indicate with small pencil tick marks a vertical plumb line about three inches from the corner, or the width of your stripes.

Step #4: Using a very straight two-by-four piece of wood, hold the four-inch side of the lumber against the wall lining it up with the pencil marks. Using a three-inch-wide mini roller, and Benjamin Moore's Latex Acrylic High-Gloss Urethane, run the roller edge down the side of the two-by-four, until a nice even coat of urethane is on the wall.

Step #5: Remove the two-by-four and line it up on the other side of the just completed wet stripe. Once again using the three-inch roller, roll down the other side of the two-by-four.

Step #6: Continue until you finish the wall(s) or room. You may notice that if the roller is too fluffy you will get a very irregular edge. If this is the "look" you want, fine; if not try the following "Not So Fast" way.

Method Two:
The Not So Fast Way

Step #1: Paint wall in the base color using Regal Wall Satin latex flat.

Step #2: Using a level, make small pencil tick marks about three inches from the first corner, creating a straight vertical line.

Step #3: Using a three-inch-wide low tack painters' tape such as Easy Mask™ or Kleen Edge™, mask down the wall, lining up the edge of the tape with the pencil marks.

Step #4: Continue over the wall, placing three or four lengths of tape. Do not tape the whole wall because the tape is reusable. It's more economical to do a few at a time and then reposition the tape.

Step #5: Using Benjamin Moore's Latex Acrylic High-Gloss Urethane and a brush or roller, paint in between the strips of tape.

Step #6: Reposition the tape and paint until the wall is completed. This way may take a little longer but the edges will be much cleaner and crisper.

Tips:

• Usually the darker the wall base color, the more the contrast will show up.

• Stripe widths do not have to be even, you can vary the width, using a one-inch and three-inch striping pattern or even work your way up from one inch to five inches and back again, creating a wave pattern.

• The best rule of thumb is to use standard tape widths as your guide for stripe widths. That way there is less measuring and therefore less chance of making a mistake.

• Keep in mind that the wider the stripes, the faster the job.

• The finish really becomes apparent on long walls — so it's great in halls.

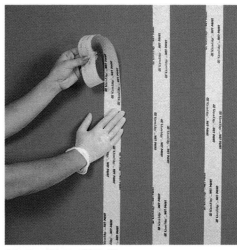

Method Two: STEP #3

STEP #5

STEP #6

PLAID —
TWO-DIRECTIONAL DRAGGING

This is a simple, casual look that is a variation on dragging, a technique explained in Benjamin Moore's FANTASY FINISHES booklet. You will need some corrugated cardboard taped to a paint paddle to keep it straight.

Step #1: Tape off all walls not to be glazed, including the ceiling, baseboards.

Step #2: Mix glaze; five parts Benjamin Moore's Glazing Liquid and one part Satin Impervo tinted to the color you want the glaze to be.

Step #3: Using a brush, paint the corner, and along ceiling and baseboards. Then roll the glaze quickly on the first four feet of wall.

Step #4: Using corrugated cardboard with one side of the outside of layer of paper removed, start at the top of the wall and pull down the wall. To keep it as straight as possible, use two hands and stand directly in front of the wall area that you are dragging.

Step #5: Continue with steps #3 and #4 until the wall is completed.

Step #6: When finished with the vertical pattern, repeat dragging process but this time start at the top of the wall and pull horizontally across the wall. To help you paint at the top of the wall, line up chairs across the front of the wall so you can walk across them. Continue dragging across wall until you reach the bottom.

COLOR TIDBITS

"There's gold in that paint can!"

When you open a can of oil-base paint that has not been shaken, why does the top of it look yellow? It's because the oil resin itself is yellow. (Look in your kitchen cupboards and you'll see the color in bottles of corn oil or peanut oil.) Stirring it well will distribute the oil throughout the paint can and the yellow tinge will disappear.

Shiny paint versus "flat" paint

The basic rule is that the shinier the painted surface, the more durable the finish. This is important to remember when painting areas that require frequent wipe-downs, such as in the kitchen, bathroom or kids' rooms.

Tips:

• You may want to have extra cardboard pieces handy in case the one you are using softens from absorbing paint.

• For the end of the wall where your piece may be too large, simply cut to the length you need to complete the wall, without overlapping areas that have already been dragged.

• Do not over-drag, if you make a mistake, use the roller to cover the mistake and re-drag, but only if it has not started to dry. Try to avoid this since doubling of the color may occur.

• Other tools to use for dragging include a squeegee, adhesive spreaders, broom, or a brush — use your imagination.

• This is the perfect look for that Ralph Lauren-influenced room.

 STEP #3

 STEP #4

SHOWER CURTAIN TO MATCH WALLS

Add dash to the bath with little cash and not a lot of work.

Step #1: Purchase two plastic shower liners, one clear and the other any color you like.

Step #2: Using either a latex or oil-base satin paint, to paint the walls the same color as the colored shower curtain, you may want to use Benjamin Moore's Computer Color Matching

System. Simply take the curtain to the paint store when you are buying the paint. The computer will read the curtain color and match it in paint. This is the base coat for the walls.

Step #3: Choose the glaze color — two shades deeper than the wall color, is an excellent choice. Have the store tint Wall Grip #1 using the paint formula. Wall Grip #1 is a clear primer for hard glossy surfaces. It will produce a translucent latex glaze when tinted.

Step #4: Roll the Wall Grip on to the largest wall as quickly as possible. You must work fast since you are working with latex which dries quickly. Imme-

diately place the back side of the clear shower curtain against the wet glaze, and *smoosh*. Remove when you are satisfied, and lay it down on the floor, flat to dry.

Step #5: In the meantime continue to smoosh the remaining walls with another sheet of plastic, which is approximately the same weight as the shower curtain.

Step #6: When the walls are dry, hang the colored shower curtain on the inside and the clear on the outside of the shower rod. Note the perfect match; actually the curtain will be the reverse pattern of one of the walls.

 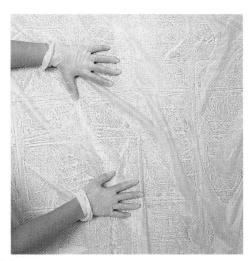

STEP #4

CRACKLE FINISH

Give an old-world look to furniture, moldings, picture frames — even walls — using new products and methods. You will need Fish Glue* and two colors of paint.

Step #1: Using either latex or oil-base paint, paint the surface with the base color. Allow to dry thoroughly.

Step #2: Dilute Fish Glue with about 20% water and using a brush, paint a thin coat on top of dry base coat. Brush on in random pattern because cracks will occur along the brush strokes.

Step #3: Leave until the surface becomes tacky — about 5 to 15 minutes.

Step #4: Apply one coat of main color of latex paint over tacky Fish Glue and allow to dry. Use hair dryer if you want to speed up the process.

* Fish Glue is available from:
   Lee Valley Tools Ltd.
   P.O. Box 6295, Station J
   Ottawa, Ontario K2A 1T4
   Telephone: 613/596-0350
   Fax: 613/596-6030
   Toll Free: In Canada 1-800-267-8767
   *   In USA 1-800-461-5053*

STEP #1

STEP #2

STEP #4

SMOOSHING

If you are searching for a marble look, here is how to get it.

Step #1: Paint the wall with Benjamin Moore's AquaGlo satin finish latex (#681). Allow to dry overnight.

Step #2: Mix glaze. Use five parts of Benjamin Moore's Glazing Liquid and one part Satin Impervo (#684).

Step #3: Apply the glaze quickly to the wall, if you think it will take longer than 10 to 15 minutes to put the glaze on the entire wall, then do it in smaller sections.

Step #4: Press a plastic drop sheet on the wet glaze; it will adhere on its own.

Step #5: Using your hands, smooth the plastic against the wall, wrinkle, rub, crinkle — anything — just move the plastic. It will probably not require more than five minutes to cover the entire wall.

Step #6: Roll the glaze on the next wall. When ready to place the plastic on the second wall, remove it from the first wall and place on the second wall.

You may have seen this smooshing technique on Benjamin Moore's FANTASY FINISHES Video but here is a new variation.

If you like the look of moiré wallcoverings or fabrics but not the price, follow the directions above but apply the glaze and the plastic as smoothly as possible to the wall. Then, starting at one end of the wall, and using the palm of your hand, gently rub down the wall, while pulling the plastic. Once you have completed that row, start at the bottom of the wall and puli up the wall, gently pulling the plastic in the opposite direction to the first row. Continue alternating up and down, smoothing and pulling the plastic until the wall is completed. Remove plastic and stand back to admire your finished faux moiré wallcovering.

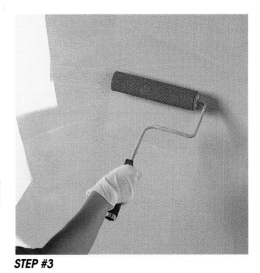

STEP #3

STEP #5

STEP #6

RAGGING -ON

This is a great finish on furniture because there are very few inside corners — only outside corners.

Draw your inspiration from something already existing in the room — fabric, a painting, or a wallcovering. Remember that it is only paint. You can always repaint if you're not happy with the results.

Be sure to use an oil-base paint if your base coat is already oil. Don't worry about filling in the chips and cracks because this technique hides all flaws.

Step #1: Paint the surface in your base color; allow to dry overnight.

Step #2: Pour your first color in paint tray. If you want a more subtle effect, the paint may be thinned with water up to 10%.

Step #3: Dip a rag (eg. cloth diaper, cheesecloth, etc.) in paint and wring out slightly.

Step #4: Using the twisted rag, start at the top of the chest of drawers and roll down to the bottom.

Step #5: Continue by rolling the next section beside the first until each side is completed.

Step #6: Apply the second colored glaze, using the same method (follow steps #3 to #5).

Step #7: Using Benjamin Moore's Latex Acrylic Urethane tinted with Benjamin Moore's White Colorant, brush a thin coat over the entire surface of the chest of drawers. This will soften the initial effect (optional).

Step #8: If not using step #7, you may want to apply a clear coat for added durability (eg., Benjamin Moore's One Hour Varnish in satin or high gloss).

Tip:
• Be sure to remove the hardware, but leave the drawers in place during painting to maintain the ragging-on continuity.

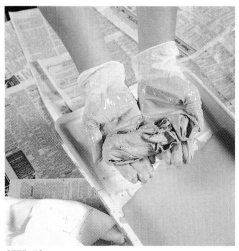

STEP #3

STEP #4

STEP #6

PEWTER FINISH

Add this elegant finish to ordinary metal occasional tables, etagères and stair railings or to up-date polished brass. It also works well on ceramic lamp bases.

Step #1: Paint the surface with a black base coat, using either Benjamin Moore's Impervo Enamel or Utilac spray paint.

Step #2: Brush a thin coat of Benjamin Moore's One Hour Varnish or Benwood Varnish on a small area to be finished.

Step #3: Using pre-mixed silver paint, dip index finger into paint (wear gloves) and randomly rub over black base in swirling directions.

Step #4: Allow surface to dry overnight. Finish with a coat of Benjamin Moore's One Hour Varnish satin finish for durability.

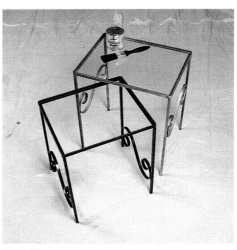

STEP #1

STEP #3

Tips:

• For larger areas, you may apply the silver paint with a brush or roller and texture with index finger.

• Only apply varnish to small sections at a time, since silver paint must be rubbed into wet varnish.

• If pre-mixed silver paint is not available, you may mix your own by using Benjamin Moore's One Hour Varnish or Benwood Varnish and metallic powders, which come in a variety of colors and are available from art supply stores.

• Use a deep green base to create a verdigris look.

TRI-ROLLER TECHNIQUE

This is one of the fastest ways to get more than one color on the wall at one time using one roller. Try combining this technique with *smooshing* or *ragging* for a multi-colored effect. You can use any type of paint: for walls, use Regal AquaVelvet or Regal AquaPearl and for *smooshing* use Glazing Liquid, mixed according to directions.

Step #1: Choose three colors to be used together. Those found on the same chip strip tend to be most successful. Paint the background of the wall one of these three colors; remove any but the lightest.

Step #2: Cut two pieces of cardboard for a paint box, giving them the same profile as the sides of your paint tray. These will become dividers in the next step.

Step #3: Using a piece of masking tape, folded along the top of the card-board divider, tape in the paint tray, so as to separate the tray into three compartments.

Step #4: Using two colors, pour at the same time, one color in each of the two outside compartments. Now pour the third color in the center compartment. Do not worry if some paint overflows into the center when pouring the first two outside areas. The center color will separate them. *(Tip: Put the lighter color in the center.)*

>

Alternative Option:
Stripes are easy to create. Use straight roller strokes down the wall.

Step #5: Quickly remove the cardboard dividers, taking care that they do not drip into the tray, since this will mix the colors. Just pull them out quickly and set aside.

Step #6: Using a roller, load the roller as for any other painting project. You will notice that the three colors will be separated on the roller.

Step #7: Start at any place on the wall, and roll the three colors in long single-direction strokes. Caution — do not use traditional back and forth roller motion or you will quickly lose your separate colors.

Step #8: Continue rolling in various directions using long swooping, soft curved edges. To get into the corners, simply run the roller's flat edge into the corner edge, and gradually swoop out towards the center of the wall.

Step #9: If more paint is to be added to the tray simply re-use dividers as before. When re-loading the roller, ensure that you put the roller back into the tray, lining up the colors, thus not inadvertently blending them.

STEP #3

STEP #8

STEP #4

STEP #6

Alternative Pattern

NEAT IDEAS

The world is filled with neat color ideas; all it takes is for you to open your eyes to what's happening around you. Take a look at what other people are doing, and adapt it to your own life. Or start an "Ideas File," clipping pictures from magazines of things that you would like to have in your home.

Turn a ho-hum hardwood floor into a work of art by painting a design on it.

To add sparkle to a previously stained floor, stencil on a design in a complementary color to the wood tone.

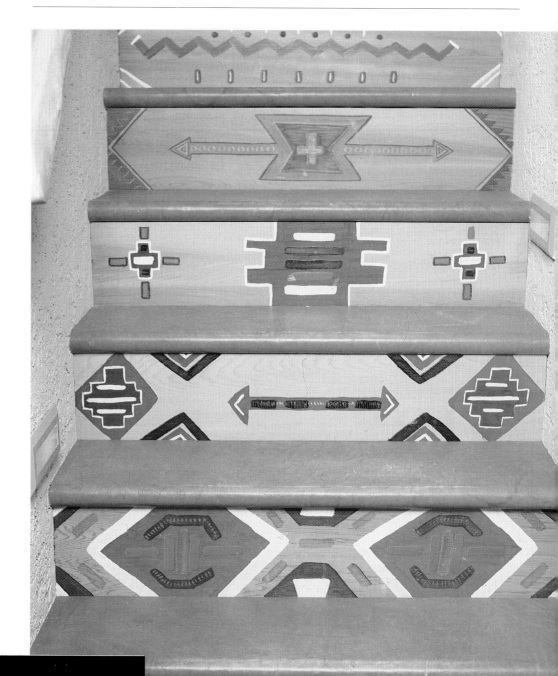

Take steps to decorate a staircase by using a combination of painting and staining. Under many ugly stair carpets a blank canvas awaits a creative touch.

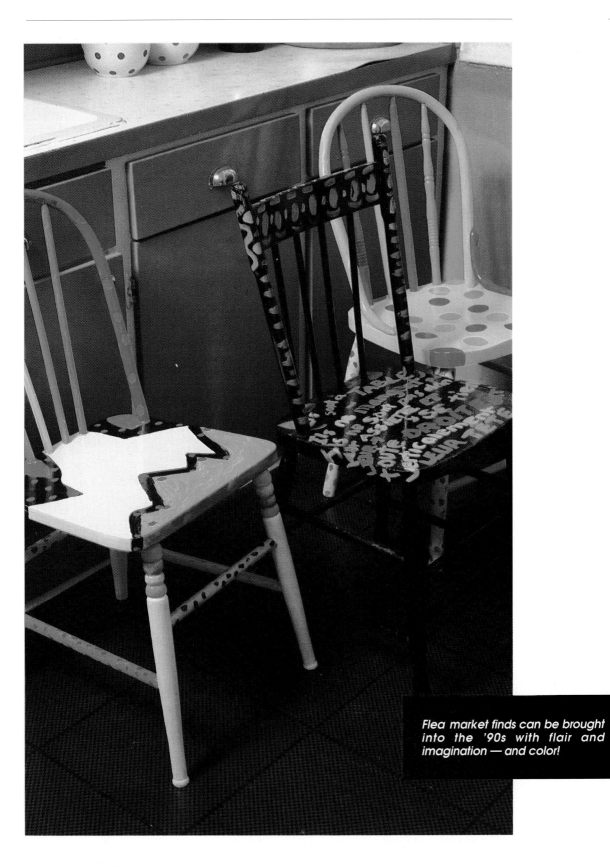

Flea market finds can be brought into the '90s with flair and imagination — and color!

Save on carpets — paint them on the floor. They won't slip and are easy to clean! Copy your ideas from the masters — or let your fancy dictate your design.

Don't be deterred by yellow tiles in a fireplace surround — paint your moldings to match. And if you don't have yellow tiles, but wish you did, you can paint the ones you already have in place.

*Up against a brick wall? Paint it —
any color you want. Latex flat paint
works best.*

Let your kids be decorators! Handprints skipping across walls are a happy touch for their very own rooms. Be sure that they use latex paint! Interior design: June Roesslein Interiors, St. Louis, Missouri.

DECORATING GUIDE

	ROOM/AREA	TYPE OF PAINT	COLOR	COLOR NO.
WALL				
CEILING				
TRIM				
WALL				
CEILING				
TRIM				
WALL				
CEILING				
TRIM				
WALL				
CEILING				
TRIM				
WALL				
CEILING				
TRIM				
WALL				
CEILING				
TRIM				
WALL				
CEILING				
TRIM				

DECORATING GUIDE

	ROOM/AREA	TYPE OF PAINT	COLOR	COLOR NO.
WALL				
CEILING				
TRIM				
WALL				
CEILING				
TRIM				
WALL				
CEILING				
TRIM				
WALL				
CEILING				
TRIM				
WALL				
CEILING				
TRIM				
WALL				
CEILING				
TRIM				
WALL				
CEILING				
TRIM				

BIBLIOGRAPHY

Birren, Faber, COLOR & HUMAN RESPONSE, New York, N.Y., Van Nostrand Reinhold Co., 1978.

Birren, Faber, COLOR PSYCHOLOGY AND COLOR THERAPY, Secaucus, New Jersey, Citadel Press, 1950, 1961.

Colby, Barbara, COLOR & LIGHT — INFLUENCES AND IMPACT, Glendale, California, Chroma Productions, 1990.

De Giandis, Luigina, THEORY AND USE OF COLOR, Englewood Cliffs, New Jersey, Prentice-Hall, 1986.

Hope, Augustine and Walch, Margaret, THE COLOR COMPENDIUM, New York, N.Y., Van Nostrand Reinhold Co., 1990.

Itten, Johannes, THE ELEMENTS OF COLOR, New York, N.Y., Van Nostrand Reinhold Co., 1970.

Kargere, Audrey, COLOR AND PERSONALITY, York Beach, Samuel Weiser Inc., 1949.

Luscher, Dr. Max, THE LUSCHER COLOR TEST, New York, N.Y., Random House, 1969.

Mella, Dorothee L., COLOR POWER, Albuquerque, N.M., Domel Artbooks, 1981.

Moss, Roger W., CENTURY OF COLOR — EXTERIOR DECORATION, Watkins Glen, N. Y., American Life Foundation, 1981.

Moss, Roger W. and Winkler, Gail Caskey, VICTORIAN EXTERIOR DECORATION, New York, N.Y., Henry Holt & Company, 1987.

Romada, Elizabeth and Larsen, Michael, HOW TO CREATE YOUR OWN PAINTED LADY, New York, N.Y., E. P. Dutton, 1989.

Sharpe, Deborah T., THE PSYCHOLOGY OF COLOR AND DESIGN, Chicago, Ill., Nelson-Hall, 1974.

Sidelinger, Stephen J., COLOR MANUAL, Englewood Cliffs, New Jersey, Prentice-Hall, 1985.

Varley, Helen, COLOUR, London, England, Marshall Editions Limited, 1983.

Whiton, Sherrill, INTERIOR DESIGN AND DECORATION, New York, N.Y., J. B. Lippincott, 1951.

Wood, Betty, THE HEALING POWER OF COLOR, New York, N.Y., Destiny Books, 1984.

INDEX

NOTES

NOTES